The Book of Glasgow Murders

The Book of Glasgow Murders

Donald M. Fraser

Neil Wilson Publishing Ltd
www.nwp.co.uk

First published by
Neil Wilson Publishing Ltd
www.nwp.co.uk

© Donald M. Fraser, 2012

A catalogue record of this
book is available from the
British Library

ISBN: 978-1-906476-04-5

Ebook ISBN: 978-1-906476-20-5

First published in April 2009.

Reprinted 2010, 2011, 2012.

Designed by Mark Blackadder
Printed and bound in the EU.

*For my late mother, Catherine Gillies and
my late father, with whom I share my name.*

*Neither lived long enough to discover that I could
string enough words together to make a sentence.*

*The book is also dedicated to my daughter Kirsty, who for
some strange reason, is an avid reader of the true crime genre.*

Contents

Acknowledgements

I take sole responsibility for any mistakes, omissions or instances of faulty logic or flawed theory in this work, as they are all mine and mine alone.

My focus for research was on the Glasgow newspapers of the day. Information was gleaned from the relevant reports in the *Glasgow Herald*, *Evening Times* and *Daily Record*. My thanks go to them.

I am also indebted to the staff and resources of the Mitchell Library in Glasgow for the use of their newspaper files.

Special thanks must go to Frank Hopson of Poole in Dorset whose family and relations lived for many years in Whiteinch, Glasgow. He was able to supply new information on the Lizzie Benjamin case (chapter 5, pages 30–38) before this book went to press.

Introduction

This is a book about murder in the 20th century in and around the Glasgow area. It tells the tales of crimes committed in streets and squares, tenements, banks, shops, parks, offices and even on the water. But it also reveals that the motive for killing a fellow human being has not really changed in that time. Murder in the 1920s was much like murder is today.

Our grandmothers and grandfathers, our mothers and fathers lived through harsh times and witnessed all manner of crime. Today, we witness the same, but in a different way. For example, major murder cases from the past could make headlines for day after day in the newspapers. In today's crowded marketplace, newspapers can hardly keep track of some cases. No sooner is it news than it is pushed into the background by another similar case the following day.

The methods of detection have also changed. When the crimes in this book were committed there was no DNA or CCTV, and in some cases, not even any fingerprint evidence. Finding out who was responsible involved old-fashioned detective work – the taking of quality witness statements and local knowledge. Tip-offs, anonymous or otherwise, also played a big part in more than one case.

Is our society of today more violent than that of our parents and grand-parents? That is a very complex question which I cannot answer here. What is absolutely certain is that when it comes to murder, there is nothing new to report in relation to both method and motive.

In order to spare the feelings of any possible living relatives of victims no cases later than the 1960's are covered. Finally, an important point. In Glasgow's defence, it has to be said that when researching this book, such was the large amount and variety of suitable material, any other Scottish city could have been quite easily selected. Glasgow does not have a monopoly on murder.

Donald M. Fraser, Old Kilpatrick, February 2009

Chapter 1

Parkhead Cross, January 1919

The Great War had finished only a couple of months previously and the euphoria of this event pervaded every feature of life for all those in the country. Hope really did spring eternal that it was the end of a war to end all wars. Loved ones were returning daily from the armed forces to a land 'fit for heroes' and the belief was that life was going to get better for all. The reality was to turn out somewhat differently.

Among the many things that had become worse during the war were the levels of crime. A number of factors were attributed to the increases. The most obvious was that the city's regular police force had been severely depleted because a large number of officers had been called up or had enlisted voluntarily. This left Glasgow Police stretched beyond its limits. Forty-two-year-old James Campbell was a married man with a wife and three young children and a veteran police constable with over 20 years service. He had remained with the police during the period of war, mainly due to his age. The younger, mostly unmarried police officers were the ones who had gone off to fight. The armed forces gain was Glasgow Police's loss.

On Saturday night, 18th January 1919, Campbell mustered along with his fellow night shift colleagues at Shettleston Police Station, in the East End of the city. As usual, much banter between the officers was the order of the day and after receiving their instructions from supervisors, the constables were ready to go and relieve their late shift counterparts. Campbell was delegated the area around Parkhead Cross as his foot patrol area, which was his regular beat, and made his way there, as usual by tramcar, to make sure he wasn't late in taking over.

Once at Parkhead Cross, Campbell spent a couple of minutes talking with fellow constable Duncan McLaglen, who was engaged on traffic directing duties at the busy five-way junction. (It has to be remembered that all of this was long before traffic lights were invented.) After his chat, Campbell walked off along Great Eastern Road, as it was called then, but is now Tollcross Road. His intention was to walk around the area of his beat at the same time as checking the security of the numerous business premises.

The vast majority of Campbell's beat consisted of tenement properties. Shops, present in most of the streets, occupied the ground level of the buildings, with offices and houses situated above them. Occasionally, smaller workshops, which were located up pends and sometimes stretched into backcourts, broke the monotony of the unending line of tenements. Checking the property, or 'pulling padlocks' as it was known, meant that Campbell would have to check both front and rear of any premises, where it was physically possible to do so.

It was just before 11pm when Campbell began his patrol. It was a typical winter's night – cold and crisp. Campbell wore his heavy greatcoat for protection from the expected freezing overnight weather. As he walked slowly along Great Eastern Road, he found everything to be secure. When he reached No 637, he knew from experience that he had to enter the close there and climb the first flight of stairs to gain entry to the backcourt, so that he could check the back of the shop premises. These were known as 'high backs', because, with the shops on the ground level of the tenement, part of them extended into the rear green areas. This meant that the backcourts of the tenement houses were actually the roofs of the shops below. It was a popularly held belief in Glasgow that houses which had a 'high back' were of a superior class to those without.

Campbell climbed the stairs and entered the darkened backcourt. Almost immediately he sensed that he was not alone. As his eyes adjusted to the dim light, Campbell caught sight of a male trying to get past him and down the stairs. Campbell grabbed the man and detained him. As he secured his grasp on the man, Campbell was about to ask him a question but stopped as he became aware of further movement within the backcourt. He saw what he thought were the shadows of three or four men moving in the enclosed area. As he peered harder, he got the impression that the shadows were climbing over a small fence that would take them into the next backcourt, and which led to houses in Westmuir Street.

Campbell didn't have the time to worry about the disappearing men. His prisoner, seeing that the officer was being distracted by the activity of others in the court, began to struggle with him, in an attempt to break away from Campbell's grasp. They grappled for no more than 30 seconds and then two pistol shots rang out. Each one reverberated off the enclosed tenement walls and made the reports boom louder than they really were. Constable Campbell released his grip on the man and slowly slumped to the ground. He had been shot once in the stomach and again just below his left ear. Warm blood trickled down his neck.

The assailant didn't hang around. He quickly vaulted the backcourt railings into the other 'high back' and made off in the direction taken by his shadowy colleagues. Almost as he was doing this, people from the street were bounding up the stairs to the rear court to see what the noises were about. These would-be helpers did not meet or pass anyone on their way up the stairs.

Once in the backcourt, they found Campbell lying on the ground, face down, and quietly moaning, 'Help me. I'm shot.' As the passers-by attended to the officer, residents came to their windows and looked out over the scene while some other inhabitants left their flats in an attempt to offer what assistance they could. One of the tenants was despatched to nearby Parkhead Cross, to inform Constable McLaglen of what had occurred and to get further assistance. When notified of the events, McLaglen ordered the tenant to go for a local doctor while he attended at the scene.

On his arrival he found that his fellow officer had been removed from the backcourt by well-meaning residents and taken to a house on the first floor in the close. Campbell had been laid on top of the kitchen table, and while lying there, spoke freely while trying to describe his attacker. A Dr Battersby, duly arrived and after a quick examination, instructed that the injured constable be taken by ambulance to the Royal Infirmary.

Campbell arrived at the hospital and was immediately admitted to a ward. Doctors consulted with surgeons but the prognosis was not good. The surgeons could not operate to remove the bullet from Campbell's neck because it was too close to his spinal column, nor could they try to remove the bullet from his stomach because the doctors could not stop the internal bleeding. Campbell's injuries were considered to be terminal. There was nothing that could be done for him, other than to make him as comfortable as possible.

As a consequence, arrangements were made very quickly to take a dying deposition from Campbell. The main element of his last-ever statement was a full description of his assailant, who was aged between 19 and 21 years of age, about 5ft 6in or 7in tall and of medium build. He was clean-shaven and wore dark clothing, which included a large thick scarf and a grey-coloured flat cap. Campbell also mentioned that he felt the presence of three or four other men in the backcourt but he could not describe them as anything other than shadows. Constable James Campbell was to cling onto his life until the early hours of Monday 20th January, when he passed away with his wife and children by his side.

By midnight on Saturday, a full-scale investigation was launched at the scene at Great Eastern Road. It was led by Assistant Chief Constable Mennie, who was head of Glasgow CID. Within a couple of hours, police had detained a suspect in a lodging-house in nearby Quarrybrae Street. It was alleged that the man, who gave an address in Blantyre, exactly fitted the description given by Constable Campbell of his attacker.

It was hoped to transport the detained man to the Royal Infirmary where he would have been confronted by Campbell from his hospital bed in an informal identity parade, but by the time this had been arranged, the officer had lapsed into unconsciousness. It was a state from which he would never recover. The man was returned to custody and he eventually appeared at the Eastern Police Court, where he was remanded for further inquiry.

On Sunday, the day after the shooting, the police made a public appeal asking for witnesses to come forward. Public attention was drawn to the fact that there was a £200 reward for information leading to the arrest of the person or persons responsible. Police also revealed that they were of the opinion that the reason for the men being in the backcourt was for the purposes of committing crime, in particular, a shop-breaking. This was hardly surprising news as the close was situated at No 637; while at Nos. 633 and 635 were the shop premises of George Young, manufacturing jewellers. One part was operated as a jeweller's while the other was used as a pawn shop. These types of premises were regularly subjected to break-ins.

During the course of that Sunday, while police were carrying out door-to-door inquires in the neighbourhood, they made another arrest. This time they detained a man, who, it turned out, was wanted for a previous assault and robbery in the Lanarkshire area. Another man was also detained in the Springburn area of the city. Both of the detained men bore a striking resemblance to Constable Campbell's description, but that appeared to be the only reason for their arrests. There was no other evidence. As a result of the police appeal, possible witnesses came forward in numbers. One man, a baker, told police of a remarkable series of events on Saturday night on board a tramcar. The man, who had just finished his shift in a local bakery, was travelling home on the top deck of a tramcar on Saturday night about 11pm. When the tram reached Parkhead Cross, a young man boarded and he appeared to be out of breath. He wasn't wearing a hat, even though it was quite cold, and he continually looked out of the back window of the tram, as if looking for someone who might have been chasing after him.

His unusual behaviour attracted the attention of the other passengers. One woman could not contain herself any longer and shouted at the man, 'Whit's wrang? Whit have ye done?' The man retorted angrily, 'There's nothing wrang wi' me.' Not put off by any means, the woman responded with, 'Where do you stay?' This type of inquisition would, under normal circumstances, be met with a less than complimentary rebuke to mind one's own business, but the man surprisingly answered, 'Wellshot Road.' He probably thought that he had quelled her interest with his response, but he was mistaken. The woman stood up, sure of herself, and snapped triumphantly, 'You don't stay there. I stay in Wellshot Road and I know everyone in it.'.

The young man knew when he was beaten and he managed to avoid any eye contact and any further conversation with everyone on the tram for the remainder of his journey, which was, for him, mercifully short. He alighted from the tramcar when it reached Wellshot Road, as did the baker, who last saw the young man walking eastwards in Main Street (now Shettleston Road) towards Shettleston. The young man's description, apart from the missing cap, matched almost perfectly with that given by Campbell and police appealed for the other tram passengers to come forward. It took almost three days of constant investigations but the police managed to trace the young man from the tramcar incident. He was able to explain that the reason for his excited and unusual behaviour on Saturday night was because he had just broken up with his girlfriend and the parting, which had taken place in the street next to Parkhead Cross, had been acrimonious. When he got on the tram, he was looking for a quiet journey to his home. Instead, he met up with a Glasgow wifie who wanted to know all his business. Police checked his story and found that it was all true. Also, he did, in fact, reside in Wellshot Road with his parents.

Two young girls came forward to say that they had seen a man aged about 20 years rushing down the stairs moments after they had heard the gunshots. This seemed to be at odds with the other witnesses who had stated that from the time of the shooting to the time of them getting to Constable Campbell's position, no one had come down the stairway. It was later decided that the girls had mistakenly identified the man who had been sent to alert the pointsman, Constable McLaglen.

The funeral of James Campbell took place during the early days of the investigation into his murder. The cortege, with full police escort, left his home in Shettleston and travelled to the village cemetery in Bannockburn, from where he originally hailed. The funeral seemed to signal an end to the story as far as the newspapers were concerned. The story of the murder of a policeman in a backcourt was soon replaced with other attention-grabbing headlines and it faded from the public's memory with indecent haste.

The murder inquiry eventually ground to a halt, although four months later, in May 1919, there was a small flurry of activity. A man was arrested on suspicion of being involved in the murder. Somewhat coincidentally, the day after his detention, a house in Govan was raided and two other men detained. These men were found in possession of a German-made automatic pistol, which was obviously a souvenir of the recent war, and all three were remanded in custody for 48 hours for further inquiry. The suspicion of involvement in the murder of Constable Campbell was lifted when it was realised that the recovered firearm was of a different calibre to that which killed the officer and two of the men were released. The third man remained in custody, charged with illegal possession of a firearm.

No one was ever brought to justice over the murder of Constable James Campbell. Nor did anyone ever admit to being involved in the incident. Unfortunately for the city, this would not be the last time that a Glasgow policeman would lose his life in the course of doing his duty and that his murder would remain unsolved.

Chapter 2
Queens Park, February 1920

Wednesday 4th February 1920 was a bitterly cold day as the two nine-year-old boys made their way along the street and into Queens Park Recreation Grounds, occasionally bouncing their football on the hard ground. The short trousers they wore only added to their feelings of cold and discomfort. Their intention was not to play on one of the small number of football pitches in the park but to use their favourite patch of grass near the park entrance for a kick-about. It was much better than the concrete playground of the Deaf and Dumb Institute, in nearby Prospecthill Road, of which they were pupils.

No sooner had they began their game when one of the young lads gave the ball a harder kick than usual, which caused it to fly past his friend and roll down a slight slope in the grass. Fortunately, the ball didn't go too far before it came to rest in a clump of bushes. The young lad bent down to pick the ball up but instead, recoiled in shock. The football had come to rest against a dead body. The two boys ran as fast as they could, back to the Institute, where they conveyed the story of their gruesome find to the first adult they met.

Very soon, the park was swarming with police, both uniformed and plain-clothes detectives. Identification of the body was going to be difficult. There were no personal papers on it, which gave the appearance of a robbery and the face of the victim had been so badly beaten that it was totally disfigured. A special note was made that the body had no shoes and that both trouser pockets had been torn away rather than just turned out. Soon, the corpse was removed to the mortuary attached to the nearby Queens Park Police Station, from where the murder inquiry would be run, and thereafter, a minute search was made of the surrounding parkland area. A number of items thought to be important to the case were recovered.

It wasn't until the following day, Thursday, that a positive identification was made. The body was that of bachelor Henry Senior, a 35-year-old stone-cutter who resided in the nearby Govanhill district with his widowed mother. She had gone to the police to report him as a missing person after he had gone out on Tuesday night, and unusually for him, had not returned by the following afternoon. Due to the injuries on the body being considered as extremely severe, it was agreed that Henry Senior's brother would formally identify his body. Even then, the identification could only be based on the clothing worn by the corpse.

Statements were obtained by police from Mrs Senior which showed that her son had left home around 7.30pm on Tuesday evening with, he said, the intention of 'meeting a girl from Fife'. He took £10 from a box on the mantelpiece but his mother chided him about carrying large amounts of cash, and to please her, he replaced most of it, keeping between two and three pounds. Although Mrs Senior became anxious when her son had failed to return home by the following day, she only began making enquiries when she read of the murder events in the local paper. From her descriptions of her son, the police were able to publicise that the deceased man was missing a pair of brown boots, an overcoat, a pocketbook, money and army discharge papers. This information led directly to the next piece of evidence in the case. A tram conductor reported to police that two men had boarded his tramcar about 9.45pm on Tuesday night in Cathcart Road, which was only yards from the area of the park. Why did the conductor remember them? One of the men had a pair of boots sticking out from his overcoat pockets, whilst the other man's hands were covered in blood. The conductor was able to provide descriptions of both men and state that they got off the tram in Gordon Street in the city centre. The police quickly realised that the descriptions provided by the tram conductor matched similar information from previously reported incidents in the park.

Acting on information, police led by Detective Chief Inspector Andrew Keith, visited numerous addresses in the Govanhill area of Glasgow. No arrests were made but thanks to more information obtained from persons interviewed at this time, the investigation took an unexpected turn. Very early on the Saturday morning, Detective Chief Inspector Keith and his colleague, Det Insp Noble, caught a boat heading for Belfast. The story of their journey was reported in the newspapers of the day and was made up of pure conjecture. Two males who fitted the descriptions of the wanted men were supposedly observed at Glasgow's Central Station boarding a boat-train bound for Ireland. It was suggested that the police were the ones who had observed this event, but, if that were the case, it would be expected that detentions would have been made at the time rather than allowing the suspects to proceed.

Once in Belfast, the two Glasgow detectives sought the help of the local

Queens Park, February 1920

force. Again, some more fanciful reporting of what followed suggested that the officers had spent all that day walking the streets, looking for the proverbial needle in a haystack and it was only when DCI Keith went for a late-night walk that he spotted two men 'who fitted the descriptions'. Keith approached the men and told them he was looking for two men like them who had committed a murder in Glasgow. Both men agreed, without hesitation, to go along to the local police station with Keith. In reality, when Keith and Noble travelled to Belfast, they had information that the persons they sought were staying temporarily in a house in Lord Street, although they did not have the exact number of the premises. The entire street had been put under observation that Saturday with no result.

By early evening, when matters were not looking promising, two men, who indeed 'fitted the descriptions', suddenly appeared from a house in Lord Street and walked off into Albertbridge Road. Keith made after them, and with the help of the local constabulary, detained the two suspects. Once back at the local police office, both detained men were interviewed. They gave their names as Albert James Fraser and James Rollins. They were stripped of their clothes, which were then taken away for examination. At first, nothing untoward was discovered until it was noticed by a sharp-eyed detective that the sleeve of the jacket taken from Fraser appeared to be cleaner than the rest of the garment. Keith slashed open the lining of the jacket and uncovered traces of blood on the inside. Even better was the discovery of a piece of paper which had the exact address in Lord Street of where both men were staying. Officers were sent there to search for any further clues. While this was going on, two females arrived on the doorstep, stating that they resided there and were the girlfriends of Fraser and Rollins. They too were promptly arrested. The names they gave to police were Gladys Renton and Elizabeth Stewart.

Keith's first problems arose with jurisdiction. He was a Glasgow policeman in a different country. It was decided that the four persons detained would be returned to Scotland as quickly as possible, so that the investigation could proceed without delay. Having been detained late on Saturday night, Fraser, Rollins, Renton and Stewart found themselves arriving at Glasgow Central Station at the ungodly hour of 5.30am on the Sunday morning boat-train from Belfast, accompanied by Keith, Noble, two Belfast detectives and two female prison warders. Word had got out about the developments in the case and, even at that very early hour, a large crowd of spectators had gathered. They vented their feelings with howls of derision as the entourage entered a police 'paddy wagon' on the railway platform and set off for the Central Police Station nearby.

9

A tight lid was put on the enquiry at this time and not much news filtered through after this except the official report that four persons had been charged with the murder of Henry Senior and would appear in court in due course. One little snippet that did make it into the newspapers was that further investigations had led the police to recover Henry Senior's overcoat and boots from a Glasgow pawnshop. They had been pawned on the day after the murder.

The full circumstances of the case were not revealed until the start of the trial, which began on 3rd May 1920 at the High Court in Glasgow. The first shock was that only the two men, Fraser and Rollins, faced a murder and three assault and robbery charges. The females who had been arrested with them in Belfast had given statements to the police regarding their involvement and had turned King's Evidence. There was the usual scramble for seats that a murder trial brings to the High Court. However, such was the interest in this case that more would-be spectators were locked out than could get into the court. Albert James Fraser, a 24-year-old deserter from the Australian army and James Rollins, a 22-year-old Irishman from County Tyrone, who was also a deserter, but from the Irish Guards, sat together in the dock. Both took great delight in the proceedings going on around them and were seen laughing and joking with each other. They were enjoying the fact that they were the cause of it all and the centre of everyone's attention.

The court first of all heard about the victim in the case. Henry 'Harry' Senior was a 35-year-old bachelor who resided with his widowed mother at 50 Robson Street, Govanhill in Glasgow. He was a veteran of the Great War, serving from the outbreak in 1914 with the 11th Hussars until he was badly injured in April 1918. By the time he recovered from his wounds, the war had finished and he was invalided out of the forces. He went back to his old employment as a stonecutter. On the fateful Tuesday night, 3rd February 1920, Senior got himself dressed up in his best clothes and, as we have read earlier, told his mother that he was going out to 'meet a girl from Fife'. When Senior removed £10 from the box above the fireplace, his mother took him to task. As a result, he replaced most of it, taking only £2 and some loose coins.

The story of what happened next is taken up in the evidence given by Helen Keenan or White, the 22-year-old female who, when she was arrested in Belfast along with the two accused, gave her name as Gladys Renton. White was told by the trial judge, Lord Sands, that whatever she might say in the witness box would not be held against her at a later date.

White first of all explained that she was an Aberdonian who came to

Glasgow about three years beforehand. She met and married a Canadian soldier who was on leave, and when he had to go back to his unit, she soon took up with the accused Albert Fraser and stayed in lodgings in the Maryhill area in the north of the city. On the night in question, both she and Fraser went into the city centre where they met up with James Rollins. She was then told by both accused to 'get a man and they would follow up'. About nine pm, White met Harry Senior in Hope Street. Without too much prompting, the couple caught a tramcar which was heading to the south of the city. White noticed at this time that both Fraser and Rollins had boarded the same tram but had sat on the outside seats.

Senior and White left the tram near to Queens Park Recreation Ground and walked into the park. After a few minutes, they both sat down on the grass next to a wooden fence. Senior produced a small pocketbook and took out a ten-shilling (50p) note, which he handed to White. It had been the agreed fee. Before much more could happen, Fraser and Rollins appeared and confronted Senior, who protested loudly at the intrusion. He was, after all, an experienced ex-soldier, and not easily scared.

Seeing the resistance offered by Senior, Fraser produced a revolver from inside his coat and pointed it at the older man. Rollins told White to go away and moved behind her unfortunate would-be suitor.

Rollins put an arm around Senior's neck and, using his knee as a lever, attempted to force his victim to the ground. Senior struggled and Fraser intervened, striking him a number of times in the face with the pistol. White told a hushed court that Senior did not shout out at all during the attack, probably because Rollins held him so tightly around the neck, and in effect, choking him. White left the scene as she had been told to do and returned to the city centre.

Fraser and Rollins continued to beat on the now unconscious man and Rollins cut Senior's trouser pockets off with a knife. He scooped up the cash as it fell on the grass. His haul was about six shillings (30p) in coins. Fraser removed their victim's boots, mainly to see if that was where Senior kept his money. This was an old trick used by, and known by, soldiers. But there was nothing. Disappointed with their meagre haul Fraser stuck the boots he had removed into the pockets of his own overcoat. Rollins forcibly removed Senior's tweed overcoat and casually slung it over his arm as both men walked off and out of the park.

It was in nearby Cathcart Road that they caught a tramcar going to the city centre and were observed by the tram conductor, who later gave their descriptions to the police. Later that night, both men met up again with

Helen White. She was given the overcoat taken from Senior and which was heavily stained with blood, and told to wash it. As it turned out, when they returned to their lodgings, it was Fraser who actually washed it and White pawned it the next morning. She got 17 shillings (85p) for it. When they met up with Rollins later that morning, he had already pawned Senior's boots, for which he received the princely sum of eight shillings and sixpence (42.5p).

Later that same day, Thursday 5th February, the three of them met up with Elizabeth Stewart, girlfriend of Rollins, and the two women went into a cinema in Argyle Street. Shortly afterwards, Fraser and Rollins appeared in the hall, agitated and frantically trying to get the females attention in the dark by waving a newspaper. Meeting them outside, the newspaper headlines showed that Senior was dead. They had murdered a man for a grand total of 41 shillings and sixpence – or in today's money – £2.07. It was decided to flee to Ireland.

At this point in her evidence, White collapsed in the witness box and spectators thought this was a well-rehearsed act. Nonetheless, the trial was temporarily adjourned. When she had recovered sufficiently some three hours later, she was cross-examined by defence counsel. White stated that she did not know that Fraser and Rollins were going to harm Senior. This remark is understandable in view of the fact that little or no violence had been used in the previous three assaults and robberies committed by this group on 23rd and 31st January and 2nd February, all at the same location. It must also be borne in mind that these were only the crimes reported to this police. Many more undoubtedly went unreported, due to their delicate nature. Awkward questions might be asked of the victim and not necessarily just by the police. Embarrassment could be a powerful deterrent.

Elizabeth Stewart briefly gave evidence also. She informed the court that on the way home on the night of the murder she noticed that one of Rollins hands was badly bruised. When she asked how that had happened, Rollins complained bitterly that, during the struggle, Fraser had struck him a blow with the revolver instead of hitting Senior. Stewart also told the court that the pistol actually belonged to Rollins and that it was, in today's parlance, a replica one. As a matter of interest, the revolver was never recovered by police. Rollins had told Stewart that he had thrown it away.

After a two-day trial and a morning of legal speeches, the jury retired. With only 20 minutes of deliberation, they returned a unanimous verdict on both Fraser and Rollins of guilty of the murder of Henry Senior and guilty on the other charges. Without any further ceremony, Lord Sands informed the pair that they *'had been convicted of an atrocious murder and there was only one duty devolving upon him'.* Assuming the black cap, the judge pronounced sentence of death on both men and set a date for the execution of 26th May 1920. Both condemned men turned to each other, smiled and shook hands. Some reports suggest that the prisoners then mocked the court, with Fraser seen wiping away pretend tears from his cheeks while Rollins drew a finger across his throat, as if slashing it, all for the benefit of the spectators in the public gallery, who were highly vociferous in their agreement of the verdict and sentence.

No matter how heinous the particulars of any crime of murder might be, there was always a petition to the authorities for the death sentence imposed on the guilty parties to be reconsidered and commuted to one of life imprisonment. In this particular case, the argument for this option was that both men went to Queens Park Recreation Ground that night with the idea of only committing assault and robbery and definitely not a murder. The appeal was rejected.

On Wednesday, 26th May 1920, at Duke Street Prison, Glasgow, Albert James Fraser and James Rollins were wakened at 6am sharp. Both ate a large hearty breakfast and, for the first time since their trial, were allowed to associate in a cell together. A small religious service was conducted by the prison chaplain and, just before eight am, John Ellis, the famed executioner, entered and pinioned the arms of both men. They made no complaint.

Fraser and Rollins then walked the short distance from the condemned cell across the landing and into the prison workshop, which housed the scaffold. After answering to their names, both stepped onto the trapdoor without any hesitation. Ellis placed a white cap over each man's head, along with a noose and stepped backwards. Just as his assistant, William Willis, was about to pull the lever that released the trapdoor, Fraser was heard to clearly say, 'Cheer up, Jimmy'. The lever was pulled and death was instantaneous for both men.

The proceedings were witnessed by, amongst others, a representative of the Australian Government as Fraser had once been a member of their armed forces, albeit briefly. It was the last double-hanging ever to take place in Scotland. Forty years later two other murderers were in trouble with the law. 19-year-old Anthony Miller and 16-year-old James Denovan were charged with murdering their victim by beating him to death in the same Queens Park Recreational Ground in circumstances almost identical to the 1920 case.

The only difference is that in the latter case, Denovan played the part that Helen White had taken in the 1920 case, and had lured the victim to a quiet area of the park with the promise of homosexual behaviour. Both Miller and

Denovan were found guilty. After a failed appeal, Miller was hanged at Barlinnie prison in Glasgow, three days before Christmas 1960. Because of his age, Denovan's sentence was commuted to life imprisonment.

Chapter 3
St Enoch Square, April 1920

Another Monday morning. That horrible feeling of the start of another long working week. It was no different for working folk on Monday 12th April 1920. Donald Smith Ross and his son, Robert Ross, both master tailors, arrived for work just after 8am at their fourth-floor workshop at 34 St Enoch Square in Glasgow city centre. They were expecting the premises to be already open for business as Mr Ross's other son, William, who held the keys to the premises, should have arrived earlier, as was his daily routine. But while access to the communal close area of the premises presented no problems, they were met with locked doors to their workshops.

Normally, the two men would have waited 20 or 30 minutes, giving their relative time to arrive, assuming his late arrival was due to a broken-down tramcar or some similar excuse. But on this day, they sent immediately for a joiner to force entry to the premises. Their fears were raised when, on reaching the last few stairs, they found William's soft hat perched on a banister post. Below the hat, a pool of blood had collected on a step and trickled down, causing a smaller pool to gather on the step below. Once inside the premises, the men were almost overcome by the smell of gas. The air was heavy with choking fumes and surprisingly, all the electric lights were on too. The men found William in the cutting room, lying on the table in the middle. He looked, to all intents and purposes, as if he had been working all night and was now catching up on some lost sleep. The reality was that William was dead. His head was resting on a makeshift pillow of a large bale of suit cloth. His head and face were covered by a ream of loose cloth, wound round and round like a turban. A piece of armoured rubber tubing was lying on the table, next to his head. The other end of the tubing was connected to the gas pipe serving the shop. Mr Ross and his son removed the cloth wrapped around William's head and found that he had been beaten badly about the face. There was an open wound on the right side of his jaw, one of his eyes was blackened and his face was extremely swollen all over. There were also a number of spots of blood on both the tabletop and on the floor in the area of the table.

15

Police were sent for and initially, they treated William Ross's death as a possible suicide. As they followed this particular line of inquiry, a number of facts came to light which caused the investigation to dramatically change direction. First, the family members who had made the tragic discovery were able to tell them that the deceased man was missing some valuables: a Waltham-make watch and gold chain and about £30 in cash. Also missing were the company's books, which William probably had in his possession over the weekend. He had previously stated his intention to write the books up on his Sunday off. Second, after the body had been removed to the Central Police Station mortuary, a postmortem examination was carried out. Death had been a result of comatose asphyxia but the corpse had other serious injuries that could be classed as being consistent with being beaten up, not least a jaw that had been fractured in two places. Also there were exceptionally high levels of alcohol in Ross's blood and the medical opinion was that he was too drunk and too badly injured to have committed suicide.

Professor John Glaister Snr was asked to visit the premises and give his opinion on all the circumstances. He found that a number of details also made suicide unlikely. The gas meter, which was religiously turned off at the end of each working day, (as was the electricity supply) was almost nine feet from the ground and therefore not within easy reach, especially for a drunk man. The large bale of suit cloth found on the table and on which William Ross's head had been found resting, was in itself, a very heavy article. It was considered too heavy for a drunk man to lift all by himself and to then manoeuvre it into the position where it was found. Added to this was Glaister's opinion that in Ross's inebriated state, he would have been unable to climb the 91 steps from street level to the workshop, without assistance. One other important factor emerged and was perhaps the most significant. The keys to the workshop were missing. So if William Ross let himself in and then committed suicide, where did the keys go?

Once it became known that the police were investigating a suspicious death, a number of witnesses came forward to tell them that just before 9pm on Saturday night, they had witnessed a taxicab drawing up outside Ross's premises followed by some unusual behaviour. When the taxi stopped, one man got out from the vehicle and entered the other door and appeared to have difficulty in removing the other passenger. Eventually, he had to call on the assistance of the driver of the cab, who then lent a hand. The two men had great difficulty in getting the third man out but eventually they did. The reluctant passenger was seen to have blood smeared across his face although it seemed to the witnesses that he was more drunk than injured.

St Enoch Square, April 1920

The man was placed against the wall, next to the close mouth leading to the shop premises. A number of times he staggered away from the wall but was caught by one of the other men. To stop the drunk from doing this again, the other men sat him down on the pavement, with his back against the wall of the building. The taxi driver climbed back into his vehicle and drove off. The man who had been assisting the drunk then walked off into Howard Street and the witnesses, by their own admission, lost interest in the events. No one could say for certain if the drunk man staggered away or maybe entered premises nearby. Just as the police were completing their statement taking, word came in that Ross's missing business books had been found. They had been hidden behind a cistern in a cubicle in the underground public toilets at the corner of St Vincent Place and Buchanan Street.

An appeal was made for the taxi driver involved to come forward but no one did. However, in this respect, the police had a piece of evidence which they had not disclosed and which they considered would prove useful in identifying which taxi had conveyed Ross to his workshop. A door handle, identified as coming from a taxicab, had been found lying in the gutter immediately outside 34 St Enoch Square. It had been picked up on Monday morning, shortly after the death of Ross had been discovered. This insignificant clue was to assist greatly in the case. As a direct result, on Wednesday 19th May, James Morrison, taxi driver was detained and then taken to the Central Police Station for questioning. He had been driving a cab that had a missing door handle.

Once at the police office, Morrison quickly admitted his involvement to detectives. He told them that he had been the taxi driver seen by witnesses removing Ross from the rear of the taxi but he denied any further involvement. Most importantly for police, he was able to name the other man involved and police immediately attempted to arrest him. Unfortunately, this man had disappeared from his lodgings. From his acquaintances, it was ascertained that he had not been seen for a number of days. Glasgow Police circulated the wanted man's details to every other police force in the UK. About a week later, information reached the police that the man they were seeking was living in Belfast. Detective Supt Andrew Keith was despatched to that city and was successful in detaining Robert Alexander Warren Halliday, a 22-year-old occasional chauffeur of no fixed abode. Keith, two RUC officers and Halliday returned to Glasgow on Friday 28th May by way of the steamer from Belfast to Ardrossan, train to Central Station and Black Maria to the police office. Halliday appeared at the city's Sheriff Court on Monday 31st May, charged with murdering William Ross and of assaulting and robbing him of money and valuables. He pled not guilty to the charges and was remanded in custody to await trial.

As Halliday was making his journey on the Friday, taxi driver James Morrison was appearing at the city's Sheriff Court, where he faced the same charges as Halliday. He was also remanded in custody until his trial. Another man, Alexander Murray, who had surrendered himself to police after Halliday's arrest, also appeared in court, having been held in custody all weekend. Murray was released from custody as all charges against him were dropped. No one is quite sure why Murray gave himself up or why he was arrested. Further inquiries were made by police in the interval between the various court appearances and the trial date. The police began dragging the river Kelvin at the bridge on Dumbarton Road, Partick. They were trying to locate the shop keys that were reported missing from William Ross's possession. The local fire brigade assisted in the search by damming part of the river and then using a pump to drain out the water. After several days, the search failed to turn up any keys and it was eventually abandoned.

Both men came to trial at Glasgow High Court on Wednesday 8th September 1920. Lord Scott Dickson, the Lord Justice-Clerk, sat in judgement in the North Court as the men were led into the dock. Both stood silently as the charge was read out to them in the following terms: that they 'Did on 10th April last, in a court at 97 West Campbell Street, in a taxicab in West Campbell Street, Argyle Street, Oswald Street, Howard Street and in St Enoch Square, assault William Ross, 49 Polwarth Gardens, Hyndland, beat him with their fists, fracture his jaw, and rob him of a watch, £30 or thereby of money, three books, four keys and a bank book.' A further charge alleged that at the premises of Ross & Company, 34 St Enoch Square, they placed William Ross, while he was in an unconscious condition, on a bench or table, turned the gas jet full on and attached a piece of rubber tubing to it and placed the other end of the tubing in his mouth and did asphyxiate him and murder him.

Evidence was led immediately at the start of the trial in an attempt by the Crown to set the tragic scene. William Ross was a 39-year-old widower and was a father to an eight-year-old daughter. He resided with his mother-in-law in the West End of Glasgow and she was able to look after the child while the murdered man went to work. He had been a member of the Royal Fleet Auxiliary during the First World War until he was invalided out after having been caught in a gas attack.

He was thought of, by all who knew him, as a quiet man with sober habits. The business was successful and there were no money worries in relation to it. Mr Ross Snr, told the court that he and his two sons had been at work on the Saturday morning. The premises were closed for the weekend just after lunchtime that day. As usual, both gas and electricity supplies were switched off and the premises locked up. William had the keys for the workshop and he was also in possession of the company books, which he stated he was intending to spend most of Sunday writing up. His father never saw him alive again.

Next up came the medical evidence. The main witness in this respect was Professor Glaister who, as stated previously, had made a detailed examination of the business premises and had also examined the dead body. He agreed with the cause of death as comatose asphyxia and further stated that while the injuries sustained by Ross prior to his death, were not life-threatening in themselves, they were serious enough to render the deceased unconscious.

Glaister pointed out that he himself was 5ft 9in tall and could only just reach the gas tap in the workroom. Having considered other witnesses evidence regarding Ross's obvious intoxication, he thought it would be impossible for him to operate the stopcock attached to the meter. Glaister was adamant that the deceased man, in his inebriated state, was unable to mentally comprehend his position and further, physically incapable of climbing the 91 steps that led to the workshop.

Dr John Anderson, one of the pathologists who had carried out the postmortem was questioned about the fractured jaw and agreed that it might have been caused by a fall on the stairway. However, he also thought that if this had happened, it would have definitely left a mark or cut on Ross's face, yet there was no wound on the body that matched.

One last witness was Lt Archibald Swan, who was in charge of Glasgow Police Hackney Branch. He told the court that Morrison's taxicab had passed its annual inspection only a few weeks before it was found with one of its door handles missing. Swan could not think of any circumstances where it could fall off accidentally. He surmised that the handle must have been wrenched off.

Before the Crown case ended, a declaration made by the accused Robert Halliday was read out to the court. The declaration had been made during one of Halliday's appearances at the Sheriff Court. In it, Halliday freely admitted robbing Ross of his money and valuables. He explained that he had met Ross about eight pm in a public house at the corner of Hope Street and Sauchiehall Street by chance that Saturday night and struck up a conversation with him. They began drinking together but Ross was thrown out for being drunk and noisy. When Halliday left the pub, he found Ross standing outside waiting for him. They walked down Hope Street together and then Halliday left Ross on his own as he went to get a taxi. He came across Morrison in his taxicab and went back to West Campbell Street and picked Ross up. Halliday said that when they arrived at St Enoch Square, Ross would not come out of the taxi as he wanted to go to sleep. Then Ross wanted a cigarette and Halliday, not having any, left to go and get some. Morrison then climbed down from his driving seat and pushed Ross out of the taxi, after which he drove off. When Halliday returned with cigarettes, he claims he found another man bending over Ross and that this man was searching Ross's pockets.

Almost immediately, this unknown man produced a key from one of the pockets and Halliday found that it fitted the door leading to the stairway to Ross's workshop. Halliday then manhandled Ross into the stairway but then, it is claimed, the drunk tailor became highly abusive towards him and Halliday decided to leave. He gave Ross his key and exited the close mouth, closing the door behind him. He never saw Ross again.

Halliday's declaration had elements of truth in it. However, there is no doubt that when the taxi arrived outside 34 St Enoch Square, Ross had already been beaten badly. All the witnesses to the events in St Enoch Square stated that one of the men was bleeding heavily around his face. Another thing that Halliday had forgotten to mention was that he and Morrison, the taxi driver, had known each other for a number of years and were good friends.

The Crown case finished and both defence agents told the court that they had no intention of bringing any evidence forward for the defence case. As a consequence, the business of summing up began.

The advocate depute told a packed courtroom that he had no option but to concur that there was insufficient evidence against Morrison in the case of the murder charge, and accordingly, he did not seek a conviction against the taxi driver on this matter.

The judge, Lord Dickson, in his summing up, was critical of the prosecution case. He stated that he could understand why they did not seek a conviction for murder on Morrison. As a taxi driver, he drove the vehicle from a position outside the passenger compartment, while the charge against him stated that he had assaulted Ross *inside* the cab, on its journey from West Campbell Street to St Enoch Square. The mere fact that Morrison and Halliday were friends did not constitute criminal activity. There was also little hard evidence to link Halliday with the murder of William Ross – if indeed it was murder. The jury would have to make that decision for themselves.

St Enoch Square, April 1920

The jury retired to consider their verdicts. It was a full hour and three quarters before they returned. Their first verdict concerned Morrison. They had unanimously found the taxi driver not guilty of all charges. Swiftly, the foreman moved on and announced that, by a majority, they found the charge of murder against Halliday not proven. This decision caused uproar in the public benches. A loud round of applause broke out and although silence was called for several times, it took more than three minutes for calm to return to the courtroom. Once it did, the foreman continued on to announce that the jury had unanimously found Halliday guilty of assaulting and robbing Ross of his money and valuables.

Lord Dickson, addressing the prisoners in the dock, told Morrison that he was free to leave, which he did immediately and without looking at his co-accused. The judge then addressed Halliday and told him that he had been convicted on three previous occasions of theft and that he considered this a very serious matter. He sent Halliday to prison to serve a sentence of five years penal servitude. Whether Halliday heard what the judge said to him is debatable. He was probably more relieved to have beaten the murder charge and avoid the death penalty. As he was led away, someone shouted 'Cheer up Alick', while a woman was heard sobbing loudly.

Robert Alexander Warren Halliday was better known to police as Alexander Warren. His previous brushes with the law had all been while using this name. During World War 1, he served in the Royal Fleet Auxiliary using that name and evidence was heard during the trial about his service record. What was also revealed was that Alexander Warren and William Ross had served in the same unit!

Could it be that the 'chance meeting' on Saturday 10th April 1920 in the pub in Hope Street was not such an accidental encounter after all?

Chapter 4

High Street, May 1921

The date was Wednesday May 4th, 1921 and the sun was shining brightly as the largest police wagon in the Glasgow Police force slowly emerged from the shadows of the covered pend that led from the yard of the Central Police Court in St Andrews Street. Its everyday job was to convey prisoners from the court to nearby Duke Street Prison, a five-minute journey up the High Street. But today was different, because it carried a special prisoner and as a result, the van was full of policemen, some of whom were armed.

Sitting up front in the open-sided cabin with the driver were two armed police officers. Det Sgt George Stirton and Det Con Murdoch MacDonald both carried fully loaded revolvers under their civilian clothes. The third officer in the cab was Inspector Robert Johnston, and although he was in overall charge of the prisoner escort detail, he was unarmed. In the rear of the van, two prisoners were ensconced in individual cells within the van and two unarmed officers, Constable George Barnard and Assistant Court Officer David Brown, watched over them. One of the prisoners had been remanded on a charge of indecent exposure, while the other was facing the much more serious charge of prison-breaking from Sligo and Londonderry jails and a further charge of stealing a firearm in Sligo. Although he had given his name as Frank Somers when arrested in Glasgow on 29th April, the police believed he was Frank J Carty, the commander of the Sligo brigade of the Irish Republican Army. Because of the serious nature of these charges, the Irish authorities had requested his extradition and Somers was remanded in custody so that this could take place.

Constable Thomas Ross, the driver of the van and a veteran of the journey, drove onto the Saltmarket and headed for Glasgow Cross. The van continued north into High Street and followed the tramlines up the gentle slope of the road. The speed never exceeded 20 mph. On reaching the junction with Drygate, which is situated on a fairly steep part of the High Street, Ross changed down gear, in anticipation of the turning and slowed to less than walking pace. What was to follow would become one of the blackest moments in Glasgow's history.

The public benches in Cathedral Square were where unemployed men met up every day to talk about whatever men talked about. No one really noticed that on this particular day, it wasn't the usual group of young men who were present. Two large groups, who moments earlier had given the appearance of milling around aimlessly, suddenly converged on the police van from the front and left-hand side. Every one of them was in possession of a firearm, either a pistol or rifle, and they all began shooting at the wagon.

Bullets tore into the area of the driver's cabin. With almost the first shot, the windscreen in front of Inspector Johnston exploded and the bullet hit him full on the chest. The force of the shot lifted him up off his seat and he slowly fell out of the open cabin, onto the running board and then slumped onto the roadway. Johnston landed on his hands and knees and remained in this position while blood spurted out of his gaping chest wound, ran between the cobbles and gathered in pools inside the tramlines on the roadway.

With all the commotion, Constable Ross had stalled the vehicle's engine and was frantically trying to restart it as bullets ripped past him. Det Sgt Stirton, having seen his colleague fall out onto the roadway injured, jumped down from his seat and stood guard over Johnston. Stirton fired his revolver at least twice before he himself was shot in the right wrist, which caused his pistol to be torn from his grasp. Det Con MacDonald was standing on the running board, firing his revolver at the many targets, which in return, were shooting in his general direction. The windscreen of the vehicle, which had been shattered with almost the first shot, was broken further with more shots and bullets tore into the surrounding bodywork.

Meanwhile, at the back of the wagon, the real reason for the attack was being played out. At least another ten men appeared at the rear of the van and began firing at its doors. One of the gunmen, described as a young lad of no more than 18 or 19 years of age, crept up close, placed the barrel of his pistol against one of the locks and pulled the trigger. Far from blowing them open, the bullet jammed in the lock and the doors remained firmly closed.

An identical attempt on the other door lock met with the same result. In an almost deadly fit of pique, or possibly in desperation, he began firing round after round into the doors and the other men followed his example. Those inside the van, two court officers and the two prisoners, dived for cover. Bullets ricocheted all around the inside of the van as the men lay on the floor. By some miracle, none of them were injured.

The murderous attack on the wagon lasted almost three minutes. Just as the assault had began without warning, so it stopped just when it seemed to reach its pinnacle. Ross was still desperately trying to restart the vehicle.

Eventually, the engine burst into life and the van moved slowly forward. This seemed to send a signal to the three groups of gunmen and almost simultaneously, they stopped firing and began running off in various directions. Three or four ran away up the High Street and were last seen in Castle Street near the hospital. As they merged in with the other pedestrians, the gunmen were seen to stuff their firearms into their coat pockets.

About ten other attackers ran off into nearby Rotten Row, chased by Det Sgt Stirton. However, he had to give up the chase after about 50 yards. His arm was bleeding heavily and a passer-by, who just happened to be a nurse, attempted to give him some first aid. As she bandaged his injured arm, Stirton said to her, 'Don't mind me anymore, go and help my chum.' Stirton was indicating towards Johnston, who was still on his hands and knees in the middle of the road.

By the time Stirton returned to the police wagon, it was moving slowly towards the prison gates and two prison guards, armed with rifles, had arrived on the scene. A passing car was stopped on the High Street and Inspector Johnston was hurriedly placed into it. The driver was instructed to take his passenger to the Royal Infirmary, which was only a couple of hundred yards away. Everyone else climbed on board the police wagon and it continued slowly through the open prison gates and into the safety of the jail yard.

Once inside the sanctuary of the prison, the van doors were found to be completely jammed. It took the combined efforts of a handful of burly prison warders to force open the doors and free the panic-stricken occupants. But Carty did not appear to have been frightened or scared by what had just happened to them.

The vehicle was examined in great detail and it was found that at least eight shots had penetrated the driver's cabin, shattered the windscreen and thudded into the wooden planking behind the seats. Another three shots had pierced the radiator, while a further six had zipped through the mudguards and bodywork at the front of the vehicle. At least a further six bullet holes were counted in and around the rear doors of the vehicle, including the two in the locks.

When everything had been completely secured, Stirton was taken to the Royal Infirmary for treatment to his wounds. As he was being seen to, word came through that Inspector Johnston had died. It turned out that he was dead even before he had reached the hospital. Johnston was 41 years of age and was a married man with two children. He had been a member of Glasgow Police since 1903. A major police operation was quickly put in place.

The police quickly formed the opinion that the attack had been carried out in an attempt to free Frank Carty. The most likely suspects would be IRA or Sinn Fein sympathisers. The investigation centred on the East End of Glasgow, probably because it contained the largest proportion of Irish immigrants. By the late afternoon, police arrested two men, who were described as being 'well dressed and intelligent looking'.

Many houses in this part of the city were searched by squads of policemen, both uniformed and in plain clothes. One of the major swoops involved the searching of the priest's house attached to St Mary's Roman Catholic Church in Abercrombie Street. Word of the raid quickly spread throughout the area and a large crowd hastily gathered outside the gates while the police were still going about their search. Soon, two men, one of whom was identified as Father Patrick McRory, were seen leaving the house in the company of detectives and were driven speedily away. The crowd of spectators immediately became aggressive and stones and other missiles were thrown in the direction of the remaining police officers. Further reinforcements were called in and they pushed back the crowds.

More houses in Abercrombie Street were searched and another five men were arrested. At one house, six revolvers and ammunition was seized. At another, in the basement cellar at 74 Abercrombie Street, an entire arsenal was found. A total of 21 automatic pistols, 12 revolvers, almost 1000 rounds of ammunition, six hand grenades, 21 boxes of gelignite and one ready-made bomb was discovered, all hidden in sacks placed in bins. It took the police nearly two days to empty the cellar, mainly because the bomb had to be diffused first.

When news of the arrests and police finds filtered back to the mobs in the East End, they went on the rampage and began smashing shop windows in the Gallowgate. Some estimates had this angry mob numbering 2,000 or more and later that evening, a number of young men from the mob attacked a tramcar as it attempted to make its way through the hordes that thronged Abercrombie Street. Almost all of the trams' windows were smashed and some of the passengers were assaulted. Police eventually managed, with great difficulty, to break up the attack and some arrests, for disorder offences, were made.

Such was the level of public disorder taking place, it was feared that a further escalation of trouble might take place, so a detachment of armed soldiers was assembled and kept on standby at the Wyndford Barracks in Maryhill. Later that night, when the large mob began rampaging in the area of the Gallowgate, many shop windows were smashed and some looting was reported to the authorities. The soldiers were then moved to the yard of the Central Police Station, where they could be deployed more quickly, if necessary. By early evening on the day of the attack, a total of 18 people had been arrested and charged with the murder of Inspector Johnson. Even so, the murder inquiry continued unabated.

On Friday 6th May, 14 men and six women appeared at the Central Police Court in private. All were charged with having discharged firearms and with wounding the two police officers, one of them fatally. With no public present in the courtroom, matters were dealt with quickly and quietly. All 20 were remanded in custody for further inquiry. One of those detained was Father Patrick McRory, the young priest from St Mary's. At the same time as these matters were being dealt with, eight men and four women were appearing in front of a magistrate at the Eastern Police Court. All of them were facing charges of forming part of a riotous crowd and general disorder. Some of them faced further charges of assaulting police officers and smashing shop windows.

Frank J Carty, whose freedom was the objective of the attack on the police wagon, was scheduled to be returned to the authorities in Ireland. A contingent of officers from the Royal Irish Constabulary was in Glasgow, and they were booked to return on the ferry sailing from the Broomielaw on Friday night, 6th May. Word had spread like wildfire and a large, vociferous crowd gathered at the Broomielaw from 7pm onwards. As a precaution, only bona fide passengers were allowed to enter the steamer shed. Any friends or relatives coming to see them off were denied access. The ferry was scheduled to depart at nine pm but just before this time members of the crew intimated to their bosses that they were not prepared to sail if Carty was on board. The ferry company cancelled the sailing and the crowd eventually dispersed.

Over the course of the weekend, Carty again appeared in court and was further remanded into custody for the purpose of being transferred into the custody of the Irish officials. On Saturday night, under the cover of darkness, Carty was secretly taken from Duke Street prison under the heavy armed escort of the Royal Irish Constabulary and via train to Holyhead in Wales, where the last part of his journey to Dublin Jail involved a voyage on a navy destroyer.

Back in Glasgow, police were still hard at work on the investigation, searching houses and arresting people. They also received two 'anonymous' letters. One purported to be from Sinn Fein, while the other suggested it was from the IRA. Both were signed, but with initials only and therefore, the authors' identities remained secret. Both letters made reference to the raid at

St Mary's Chapel and the arrest of one of the priests. Their anger was centred on the allegation that armed police officers had entered the chapel itself and threats of retaliation were made in relation to named police officers. However, the chief constable himself, Mr JV Stevenson, issued a denial via the newspapers, stating that the officers involved did not enter the chapel, only the chapel house. Inspector Johnston's funeral also took place on this weekend. The cortege left his home in Shettleston and was escorted by uniformed police all the way to the outskirts of the city. The procession then continued to Castle Douglas in Kirkcudbrightshire, Johnston's birthplace, and where he was later buried in a local graveyard.

By the end of the second week of investigations, a total of 34 persons were being held in custody in connection with what the newspapers of the day had described as the 'High Street Outrage'. Not all of those detained were charged with murder. Some were charged with alleged acts in relation to Sinn Fein activities. During their inquiries, police discovered that there was a high possibility that one of the attackers of the police wagon had been shot, and although he had been helped away from the scene, it was alleged that he later died from his wounds. Police appealed for information from the public for assistance in finding out if the rumour was true or not, for, as they pointed out, the attacker's death was unlikely to be reported to them in the normal way. Needless to say, no information came to light.

The police continued with their inquiries. All through the month of May, people were arrested, charged, appeared at court, and on some occasions, were released from detention. By the last day of the month, a total of 37 men and women had been subjected to charges involving the murder of Inspector Johnston. One female, Margaret Dawson or Quinn, an 18-year-old from the Parkhead area of the city, carried her three-month-old child as she stood in the dock. When she was remanded in custody, her child went with her to jail.

In an effort to avoid scenes of unnecessary disorder and allegations of bias and prejudice, the trial was moved to Edinburgh High Court. By the time it started on Monday 8th August 1921, only 13 of the 37 accused persons were still facing charges. Lord Justice Clerk, Lord Scott Dickson presided over the hearing and it was expected to last ten days; 138 witnesses were cited to give evidence for the Crown and there were a total of 340 productions in the case. Unusually, 200 possible jurors were summoned to the courthouse and this meant that there was no room whatsoever for any members of the public to gain access and listen to the proceedings. A jury of seven women and eight men was eventually empanelled and they spent every night of the trial in a hotel at the court's expense. Large crowds gathered every day of the trial but they were kept from encroaching into the precincts of the courts of justice by a high number of police officers. The following prisoners squeezed themselves into the dock: James Mitchell also known as Joseph Dunne, Daniel Branniff also known as Charles Grier, James McArra, John McGarrigle, Vincent Campbell, John Carney, William Fullarton, James Fullarton, Michael O'Carroll, Lean O'Daire, James Kavanagh, Thomas Tracey and Francis O'Hagen.

All of the accused faced two charges. First, that they were involved in the murder of Inspector Johnston and the attempted murder of Det Sgt Stirton, and second, that they conspired, with others, to further the objects of Sinn Fein by the unlawful use of force and violence, especially by means of explosives and firearms to the danger of lives, property and persons. Each defendant lodged a special defence of alibi.

Everything proceeded as had been expected during the first week of the trial. Witnesses turned up and gave their evidence without any major controversy. On Monday 15th August, as the second week of the trial got under way, one of the accused was seen to be missing from the dock. Francis O'Hagen had become unwell over the preceding weekend and had been certified insane and unfit to stand trial. The court heard evidence from medical experts that O'Hagen was 'quite incapable of giving further instructions for the conduct of his defence.'

In light of this information, the Crown asked that they be allowed to desert the case against O'Hagen but proceed with the case against the other accused. This was agreed to. Again, another full week of witness after witness was heard. Towards the end of the week, the witnesses were for the defence and concerned their special defence of alibi. Evidence was heard which stated that each accused man was elsewhere at the time of the attack on the police wagon.

By Saturday lunchtime, all speeches by the crown, the defence counsels and the judge's summing up had been heard. At 1.35pm the jury was instructed to retire to consider their verdict. Back in Glasgow, police were also on standby, awaiting the jury's verdict. Their decision could mean the difference between peace and quiet or an all-out riot in the East End of the city. It took them almost 90 minutes to announce that they had reached a decision; just after three pm they declared that they found both charges against Mitchell, Grier, McArra, Campbell, Carney and William Fullarton not proven and in the case against McGarrigle, O'Carroll, O'Daire, Kavanagh, Tracey and James Fullarton they returned not guilty verdicts on both charges. The jury were thanked for their long service in the trial and

Lord Scott Dickson told them that, as a thank you for their service, they were all to be exempt from sitting on another jury for the next ten years.

While those in the dock celebrated, shook hands and clapped each other on the back, they failed to notice Det Lt Noble entering the group and singling out Mitchell. Within seconds, Mitchell was in handcuffs and being led down to the cells below. Unbeknown to anyone, apart from a few senior police officers, two prison warders from Strangeways Prison in Manchester had been allowed into the courtroom during the trial's proceedings. They positively identified Mitchell as a man known to them as Daniel Patrick Walsh, who had escaped from the prison in October 1919. Therein lay the reason for his re-arrest.

It appears that there was no justice in the case of the murder of Inspector Robert Johnston. Those who had stood trial were now free. The police inquiry did not continue. The authorities were happy that they had arrested the murderer and put him on trial. They did not think it necessary to re-open the investigation.

Yet, one part of the investigation left a question that begs an answer. During the inquiry, the police sought to arrest three men, who they named as Frederick Quinn a 21-year-old from Edmiston Street, Parkhead and Aimon Mooney (23) and his younger brother, Sean Mooney (19), who resided together at 1 Shaw Street, off Garscube Road, in the Maryhill area. All three were known members of Sinn Fein and police were so desperate to detain them, they had photographs of the wanted men published in the daily newspapers. Even so, they were never arrested. Could it be that they had had some bearing on the case?

The murderer of Inspector Robert Johnston remains unknown to this day.

Chapter 5

Whiteinch, November 1921

Although she was four months short of 15 years old, she was well built and could have passed for older. She was described by most people who knew her as a happy carefree girl who had a kind word for everyone she met. So why was she found dead on a cold and wet November morning, lying in a Glasgow backcourt with her head and face smashed in?

Elizabeth Benjamin was employed by her elderly father to collect orders and payments from customers in the Scotstoun and Whiteinch areas of the West End of Glasgow in 1921. She was a door-to-door saleswoman who carried drapery items like handkerchiefs, blouses and lace place settings (doilies) in a small black suitcase and kept her collected money payments in a red leather purse.

On Monday 31st October 1921, Elizabeth set out from her home at 1 North Elgin Street, Clydebank, on her usual weekly round of customers. Firstly, in the morning hours, she visited houses in the Scotstoun district. All of this went as normal. The afternoon found her calling at homes in the Whiteinch district. About three pm, she was in a house in the tenement property at 67 George Street. She collected a small amount of money as a part-payment on account and then left to visit another house directly across the street at No 88. During her conversations with the occupants she mentioned that business had been very slow that day. By way of confirmation, Elizabeth explained that she had brought along £2 in coins in order to give customers change from their payments, but she had had no occasion to use it. Elizabeth then stated, as she left, that her next house call was to be in nearby Dumbarton Road. She never made it to the next house. Elizabeth vanished completely.

Just before seven am the following morning, a female resident at 67 George Street was working away at her kitchen sink, which overlooked the backcourt. Through the gloom of a grey morning, she thought she could make out the shape of a young boy lying on the damp ground, against a stone wall. She went out to investigate only to find a battered body. She then ran and hammered on the door of her neighbour. After telling of her grim discovery, the two women scurried along the street to the local police office, which was no more than 200 yards away in Oswald Street. An officer was despatched to the scene and almost immediately he called for further assistance as he realised that he was dealing with a murder.

The body was dressed in a brown overcoat, blue dress and black long-legged boots (which looked like trousers from a distance). Although there appeared to be very little blood on the ground, the young girl's head had been severely bludgeoned, causing major damage and a large wound ran across her forehead and down the side of her nose. Both her hands were lifted above her head and were tied together at the wrists. It was later found that the rope used was similar to the type used to tie down tarpaulins that covered railway wagons and that the knot used was a 'clove hitch', which is more commonly used by sailors.

Detective Superintendent Andrew Keith, who was also involved in the Queens Park murder case (see chapter 2), was called to the scene and took charge of the investigation. He decided that door-to-door enquiries needed to be carried out without delay along with a detailed and thorough search of the entire neighbourhood. This was no mean feat when it is considered that the houses of the neighbourhood were all tenement properties, some five storeys high and most with at least three flats per storey. To effect this he drafted in almost 100 detectives, taken from every police office in the city. Other police officers, given the task of the detailed search, enlisted the help of a number of unemployed local men, who had been doing nothing else other than form part of the large crowd that had squeezed into George Street and then stood around, silently watching developments.

Elizabeth's failure to appear for the family evening meal aroused suspicion but her relatives did not contact the police. Instead they carried out their own search. Houses of friends and acquaintances were visited but no one had seen or heard from Elizabeth. It was the following morning before they found out what had happened to her when the police called at the family home and asked them to attend the murder scene. Once there, they officially identified the girl's body as it lay in the cold mud.

When detectives ordered the body removed from the scene, it was noted that the ground under the corpse was bone dry, suggesting that the body had been there before it had started raining in the early hours of the morning. It was also observed that there was a distinct lack of blood at the scene, nor was there any sign of a struggle evident in the muddy ground. Muddy footprints and some bloodstains were found on the coping stone on the top of the wall, indicating that those responsible had climbed the wall to make good their escape.

The residents at No 67 were among the first to be interviewed. One resident, a woman, stated that she heard voices outside at a very late hour, but it did not seem to be unusual and she did not make any further investigation. Another female resident, from the top floor, said that about three am she had occasion to look out of her window and could make out a faint shape lying in the backcourt. She thought it was a 'Halloween dummy' and went back to bed.

Within a couple of hours, the search parties had turned up some vital evidence. An ashpit in a backcourt, a number of closes away from where the body was found, was discovered to have a substantial number of pieces of linen cloth in it. All of the linen was bloodstained, wet or partly burned, or a combination of all three. Detectives at once swooped on the tenement property. Occupants of the houses were quizzed and their homes searched. However, at one flat on the ground floor, the police could not get an answer to their repeated knocking. Just as a decision was made to force an entry, the door slowly opened. Inside, were found two men and a woman who admitted that it was she who had thrown the linen into the ashpit and she had found a black suitcase on her back window ledge earlier that morning. Knowing exactly what it was, as word of the discovery of the body had spread quickly through the neighbourhood, the three occupants feared not being believed and decided that the best way to dispose of the suitcase was in the fireplace. Unfortunately, the contents were soaking wet and wouldn't burn properly. The men cleaned out the fireplace and the ashes were thrown in the backcourt pit. There were about to destroy the suitcase when the police called.

All three were arrested and taken to the Central Police Station for further questioning. The men were brothers and the woman was the wife of one of them. They were all about 30 years of age. Very quickly, the police realised that what their prisoners had told them was, in fact, the truth. They had nothing to do with the actual murder of the Benjamin girl. Subsequently, on Wednesday 2nd November, all three were released from custody. However, it was not down to the interrogation methods of the police that proved their innocence but more the fact that the officers had received startling information which not only corroborated the detained persons stories but also led their enquiries off in a different direction.

The information provided led police to a house No 67 George Street, where, during a meticulous search, the metal framework of a red-coloured purse was found in the ashes of the fireplace of the house. As the search continued, so more evidence came into focus. Bloodstains were found behind the front door of the flat, on the floor, walls and the door itself. A large drill bit, 18 inches long by one inch in diameter, made of solid grooved steel and covered in blood, was found in a hallway cupboard. Once more, the police arrested the occupants of the house – again, two brothers and the wife of one of them – and took them to Partick Police Station. Their names were given as John Harkness, aged 33 of 83 Douglas Street, Partick; William Harkness, aged 31 of 67 George Street and his wife Helen McCleary or Harkness, aged 28 years. The woman was also known locally by the name Nellie. As they languished in custody, the search of their property continued. In the communal washhouse at 67 George Street, police found a heavily bloodstained zinc bath in a corner. When it was lifted up, the floor underneath was bloodstained too.

A postmortem examination was carried out by the eminent Professor Glaister, who found that death was due to asphyxiation. While Benjamin had been severely beaten and these injuries were extremely serious, they were not, in themselves, likely to have been fatal. Glaister found a white linen handkerchief lodged in the girl's throat. It had been the cause of her death. Glaister also estimated that the time of death was around four pm on 31st October.

On the afternoon of Thursday 3rd November, a large crowd gathered outside Partick Police Station, to silently pay their final respects to Elizabeth Benjamin. Her funeral cortege, consisting of a hearse and two coaches, left there and travelled to Sandymount Cemetery in Shettleston. The following day, at the same police office, a huge throng of people formed up outside. The doors to the courtroom were opened and a scramble for seats in the public benches took place. Even so, more than 500 were still left outside. The three prisoners were brought through from the cells and stood quietly in the dock. The charge was read out: that in the house at 67 George Street or elsewhere, they did assault Elizabeth Benjamin and murder her. As the clerk finished reading the charge, Mrs Harkness fainted but was saved from falling to the floor by a quick thinking wardress, who caught her and took her back to the cells.

All three accused were remanded in custody, and this time, removed to Duke Street Prison. As the prison wagon left the yard at Partick Police Station, the crowd surged forward and banged on the sides of the vehicle. Screams of derision and shouted threats continued until the wagon disappeared into traffic.

Almost exactly three months later, on January 30th 1922, two of the accused, William Harkness and his wife Helen, went on trial at the High Court in Glasgow, accused of Elizabeth Benjamin's murder. The charges against the third accused, John Harkness, had been dropped and he was cited to appear as a witness. And what a witness he would turn out to be! The trial created a stir in Glasgow. While it lasted only two days, it attracted thousands of people eager to get a place in the courtroom. Those that didn't, milled about the precincts of the courthouse and on nearby Glasgow Green.

The trial started with a procession of female witnesses, all residents of various addresses in the Whiteinch area and all customers of Elizabeth Benjamin. They gave evidence as to when she called on them and when she left. What this established was that the murdered girl left Mrs Graham's house at 88 George Street about 3.35pm that fateful day and was never seen alive again. Next into the witness box came six female residents of 67 George Street, all neighbours of the accused. Some witnesses spoke of finding what looked like bloodstains in various places on the common close stairs, including the doorstep of the Harkness's flat. Other neighbours stated that they saw both accused in the washhouse on the evening of October 31st.

Next came the most sensational part of the trial. John Harkness, brother of the accused William, gave evidence. He told the court that he was in the home of his mother-in-law at 1204 Dumbarton Road when Helen Harkness called about 8pm on October 31st. She was reeking strongly of alcohol as she asked him to go with her and meet his brother. She would only say that there had been some trouble. Harkness agreed and went to 67 George Street, where he met his brother, William. When he asked his brother what trouble he was in, William replied that he had hit a woman over the head and killed her. John Harkness was then taken to the washhouse and, by candlelight, shown the body of the dead girl lying in a far corner of the darkened building. Helen Harkness allegedly said at this point that the girl only had £1 in her possession, but if they had done in the factoress (female rent collector), they would have got nearly £50.

William Harkness asked his brother to help him to get rid of the body from the washhouse and he agreed. They quickly removed it and placed it in the backcourt, in the place where it was later found. William Harkness began clearing up the washhouse, using a bed mat and old clothes to wipe up the bloodstains from the floor, but this was not particularly successful. He then decided to cover up the stains by throwing the contents of a bucket of coal dross over them.

John Harkness took the bloodstained bed mat and clothes and threw them into the ashpit at 69 George Street and then went back to the home of his brother. As he entered, he was met by a blanket of thick smoke. He found that it was coming from a metal pail placed in the hearth of the fireplace. His sister-in-law Helen was burning some pieces of cloth and books. She then produced a suitcase that had belonged to the dead girl and stated that she intended to burn that as well. She was stopped from doing this by John Harkness, who at first argued with the couple but then agreed to dispose of the item for them.

On leaving the house, John Harkness walked along George Street a short distance then darted into a close mouth. He discarded the suitcase in the backcourt, climbed the railing and exited out onto Dumbarton Road and walked to his mother-in-law's house nearby. At one point, John Harkness thought about calling in at the local police office, but because his brother was involved, he decided otherwise. Somewhat strangely, once back home, he told his mother-in-law, Mrs Tolland, everything that he had seen and done.

Not until the following day, when the crime had been discovered and reported in all the newspapers, did John Harkness call at his brother's house. He wanted to remonstrate with his brother about the fact that the dead girl was only 14 years of age and she had been gagged. However, when he brought the matter up, he told the court that Helen Harkness retorted, 'Yes Johnny. She was a tough little bastard. My legs are all black and blue where she kicked me.' His brother boasted that he had been bitten on the fingers by the murdered girl.

Sometime later that day (November 1st), detectives arrived at the house and all three were arrested. John Harkness made a voluntary statement and cleared himself from any major involvement in the murder. His statement was eventually corroborated by other evidence. However, he still faced charges involving assisting in disposing of the body and of some evidence. At a later date, he agreed to give evidence in return for immunity from prosecution. It was revealed in evidence that police knew what house to go to after receiving information from Mrs Tolland. She had been told of the discovery of the dead girl's body whilst at work and on her return she immediately went to the police and told them what she had been told by John Harkness the previous evening.

On the second day of the trial, the Crown case was concluded around midday. No witnesses were called for the defence, and after hearing speeches from the relevant counsel and the judge's summing up of the evidence, the jury retired to consider their verdict at 2.55pm. The feeling of tension and hostility was clearly evident in the courtroom. Earlier, at the lunch break, John Harkness had been set upon by a number of men and assaulted as he ate his lunch in the courthouse restaurant.

The jury returned 30 minutes later at 3.25pm with two unanimous verdicts of guilty of murder on William and Helen Harkness. The jury however, stipulated that they strongly recommended mercy be shown to the female prisoner. The judge, Lord Hunter, addressed the husband and wife as they stood together in the dock. The prisoners held hands with each other as he sentenced them to be executed at Duke Street Prison on 21st February. John Harkness, who had been sitting at the back of the courtroom, jumped onto his feet and screamed, 'Oh Willie, Willie', just as a woman sitting near the front of the courtroom fainted. Helen Harkness began sobbing uncontrollably. Her husband showed no emotion whatsoever but gently patted her on the back as both were quickly led down the stairs to the cells below.

The true story of the events that befell Elizabeth Benjamin are arrived at by the process of combining testimony, circumstantial evidence and medical fact and opinion together. On leaving 88 George Street, the young girl was intercepted by Helen Harkness and asked to go the flat at 67 George Street under the premise of the Harkness's wishing to purchase some of her wares. Once there, Elizabeth showed off her samples but with no sale forthcoming, she was eager to leave and proceed with her calls. As she walked along the hallway towards the front door, William Harkness struck Elizabeth on the back of the head with the reamer, causing her to fall forward against the back of the front door. Helen Harkness then jumped on the stricken girl, holding her down while her husband struck more blows with the reamer. In the struggle, Elizabeth fought bravely for her life. William Harkness decided to quieten the screaming girl and forced a handkerchief into her mouth, although she didn't make it easy for him. She bit him hard on his fingers, drawing blood. But with the overwhelming force of two adults against her, the young girl had no chance of survival.

Later that evening, Helen Harkness asked one of her neighbours if she could borrow the key to the communal washhouse, which was situated in the backcourt. Then, along with her husband, they placed Elizabeth's body in a zinc bath and carried it down the stairs and secreted it in the outhouse. They were both observed in the washhouse by a neighbour about 6.30pm. Knowing that if the body were to be discovered in the washhouse, the finger of suspicion would quickly point to them, they took Elizabeth's money and headed to a nearby public house in Dumbarton Road. In the pub, they discussed their predicament and decided to involve John Harkness.

The recommendation of mercy from the jury was directed to the proper authorities and on Saturday 18th February, a dispatch from the Scottish Office was received at the prison by the governor, Mr Drysdale. It contained the information that Helen Harkness had been reprieved from the death sentence and that it had been commuted to one of penal servitude for life. In the same communiqué, it stated that the Secretary for Scotland was unable to interfere with justice in the case of William Harkness and his execution was to proceed as planned. William Harkness was visited in his cell and told of the decisions. He never uttered a word or showed any emotion. He stared blankly ahead. When Helen Harkness was told of the news, her eyes filled with tears.

One minute before eight o'clock on Tuesday morning, 21st February 1922, John Ellis, executioner, entered the condemned man's cell. After confirming his name, Harkness' arms were pinioned to his sides and he was slowly marched out of the cell, across the landing and into the prison joiner's workshop, where the scaffold had been erected.* He stepped onto the trap door and a hood was immediately placed over his head and face, then the noose was adjusted around his neck and the lever pulled. Harkness fell to oblivion and was dead a moment after the rope stiffened and jerked. The black flag was hoisted above the prison at one minute past eight. Several hundred spectators had gathered in the surrounding streets in the cold, wet and blustery winter morning since around seven am, watching the arrival of officials. As soon as the flag was seen, the crowds quickly and quietly dispersed.

Helen Harkness was released from prison on 16th March 1937 and, like other prisoners before and after her who had been found guilty of a heinous crime, tried to quietly disappear from public view. However, she was convicted twice in the next ten years on theft charges and served a prison sentence for each. Her last dealings with the law came on 30th October 1947 when she was released from custody.

George Street no longer exists in name, likewise Oswald Street and Gordon Street. Residents of the area, past and present, will now know them better as Medwyn Street, Inchlee Street and Glendore Street respectively. Whiteinch was part of the Royal Burgh of Govan up until 1912, when it was incorporated into the boundaries of Glasgow. Because Glasgow already had streets named George, Oswald and Gordon, (all in the city centre), those in Whiteinch were changed in 1931 to what they are known as today.

The reamer with which Harkness bludgeoned his victim to death is a tool used in shipyards for enlarging holes in the iron plates of a ship before they are riveted together. William Harkness worked for A&J Inglis, shipbuilders of Meadowside, Whiteinch at the time of his arrest. Curiously, a few years

---

* There was no dedicated execution room or chamber in Duke Street Prison.

prior to this case, another woman was murdered in the vicinity, this time at her place of employment at Oswald's Dairy, Dumbarton Road, Whiteinch. Miss Lucie McArthur was found behind the counter of the shop; she had been beaten to death as she opened the premises in the early hours of the morning ... her hands had been roped together at the front of her body with a 'clove hitch' knot. That case remains unsolved to this day.

John Harkness met a gory end when he was found in the backcourt of 1188 Dumbarton Road, Whiteinch, in the early hours of New Year's Day 1927. He was suffering from serious injuries, including a skull fractured in many places. Those injuries led to his death later the same day. Police opinion was that he had fallen or had been pushed from a great height. A local male resident was arrested on suspicion of murder but later released without charge due to insufficient evidence.

Chapter 6
Coatbridge, June 1923

During the course of the 20th century, only 15 women were hanged in the United Kingdom. Of them, just one, Susan Newell, suffered the ultimate punishment in Scotland. This is how she came to find herself on the scaffold.

Susan McAllister was born in Oban in 1893 into abject poverty, an aspect that never really changed for the rest of her life. After completing school, at which she never excelled at anything in particular, she found a succession of menial low paid jobs in the highland port. By 1910, Susan was 17 years old and eager to escape what she considered her restrictive surroundings. She boldly moved to the metropolis that was pre-war Glasgow and got herself a job. Susan seemed to have been making a go of her new life, despite the fact that her employment was no different to when she was in Oban. In 1914, she met and married John MacLeod, a 24-year-old from the Isle of Lewis, who like her, had come to the big city to find his way. History does not record whether Susan and John had a happy marriage and at the outbreak of the Great War, John immediately signed up and was sent overseas. Susan was left all alone, but not for long. Early in 1915, she gave birth to their daughter, whom she named Janet.

Within months of the birth, Susan received devastating news. Her husband had been killed during trench warfare in northern France. He never had the opportunity to see his daughter and what became of the little baby and her mother is not known until 1922, when the story restarts. By now, Janet had grown into a mischievous seven-year-old while Susan was approaching 30 years of age. She met, fell in love with and married 29-year-old John Newell, who resided in the small Lanarkshire village of Summerlee. He was employed as a tubeworker at the British Tubeworks in nearby Coatbridge. At first, everything seemed fine. Susan, John and Janet lodged with relatives in the small village, but within months matters took a downward turn. First, just after Christmas 1922, John lost his job, along with many others, thanks to lay-offs at the factory. With so many local workers looking for alternative employment at the same time, John failed to get another job. For six whole months he was out of work. Tempers became frayed between the couple and between themselves and their relatives with whom they resided. The common factor in the many disagreements was the excess consumption of alcohol by all concerned.

At the start of June 1923 one argument too many led to the family leaving Summerlee and moving into lodgings at 2 Newlands Street, Coatbridge. The new surroundings did nothing for their happiness and the infighting continued. On Tuesday 19th June, during a particularly heated exchange, Susan attacked her husband. It wasn't the first time she had done so, but on this occasion she left his head and face bloodied and bruised. He felt upset about it enough that he called at the local police station and reported the fact that his wife had assaulted him. Due to a lack of evidence, and a possible reluctance to become involved in domestic disputes, the police did not even speak to Susan Newell about the allegations. Fearing a repetition or worse, John Newell packed his bags and left his wife and stepdaughter. After all this, Susan still had one last blow to come her way. Her landlady, Mrs Young, gave her notice to quit the lodgings by the coming Saturday, the excuse being her unacceptable behaviour.

The following day, Wednesday 20th June, was carnival day in Coatbridge. The annual Old Monkland Agricultural Show, with its attendant side-shows and attractions, took place at local Dundyvan Park. Thirteen-year-old John Johnston was well known locally. He was a street newsvendor, selling his daily papers in all weathers. The show in the park gave him an ideal opportunity to sell more than his normal amount. Even so, he still did not forget his regular customers, and he called at Newlands Street and began knocking on the doors of the houses, hoping to sell his papers. At about 6.45pm he stood on the doorstep of No 2. Mrs Young invited him in as usual and he immediately called at the door of Susan Newell. Mrs Young entered her own part of the house just as the Newell's door was opened to young Johnston. She heard nothing else but assumed he had sold his papers and moved on.

The young lad was invited into the flat and once inside, Susan took a newspaper from him. However, she made no attempt to pay for it and an argument ensued between the pair. The disagreement ended very quickly with John Johnston lying dead on the couch, his newspapers strewn over the floor. He had been strangled. Irrespective of whether Susan Newell was drunk or in a blind rage, she soon reverted back to her normal self. Just before 7.30pm, she met Mrs Young in the communal kitchen of the lodgings. She asked her landlady if she could borrow a large box in order to pack some items prior to her leaving. Mrs Young told Susan that she had such a box but would have to wait until the following morning to get it. This seemed to be agreeable to Susan and the matter was left at that.

Just after this, eight-year-old Janet arrived at the flat; she had been out playing with friends. The scene that confronted her of the dead body of the newspaper boy lying on the couch must have been extremely difficult for a young child to comprehend. Susan swore her daughter to secrecy and cajoled the youngster to help her wrap up the body in a rug. About 8.30 that evening, both mother and daughter left their lodgings. Where they went, no one knows. They both returned just before midnight. About five minutes later, Susan Newell was seen leaving her flat, without her daughter and did not return until 1.30am. Once more, minutes later, Susan departed the house only to finally return an hour later. The movements of Susan Newell are a matter of record, thanks to the keen eyes and ears of her landlady, Mrs Young. However, not even her nosiness could detect exactly when Susan Newell left the house for the last time that morning. It was sometime before 8am as there was no answer to repeated knocking from Mrs Young. Unbeknown to her, at that very moment, her lodger and daughter were seen pulling a child's go-cart in nearby Dundyvan Road. The cart seemed difficult to move as it was fully laden with what appeared to be clothing.

There were no more reported sightings of Susan and her daughter until 9.30am at a road junction in Bargeddie. Thomas Dickson, a delivery driver for a local fruit merchant, stopped his lorry when he saw two women and a child walking at the side of the road. One of the women asked Dickson if he could give the other woman, her child and go-cart a lift into Glasgow, as they were going to look for digs. Dickson agreed. He helped lift the cart onto the rear of his lorry and then drove off towards the city.

Susan and Janet sat in the cab of the lorry and never uttered a word during the entire journey. Half an hour later, as the vehicle trundled along Duke Street in Glasgow's East End, Dickson turned to Susan and suggested that she got out and looked for lodgings in the general area. His thinking was that the East End was a working class area and that it would have accommodation within Newell's obvious price range. Dickson stopped his lorry outside Parkhead Forge and climbed onto the flatbed area. He began to push the go-cart off the edge of the vehicle, into the hands of Newell, who was standing on the pavement, arms outstretched. Unfortunately, the weight of the go-cart was too much for Susan and it almost turned over and fell to the ground. Dickson managed to catch hold of the cart, which stopped it from falling completely, but the bundle inside it became partially dislodged.

John Johnston's head protruded from under the thick quilt-like cover, while his left foot jutted out at the bottom, hanging loose over the end of the cart. Newell quickly recovered her grip on the go-cart and hastily shrouded her grisly cargo. She thanked Dickson for his efforts with a terse, 'I'll manage it. Leave it alone.' Susan and Janet then turned away and walked off along Duke Street. But the damage had been done. The incident had been witnessed by an alert resident, who in typical Glasgow tenement fashion, had been 'windae hinging' (leaning out of one of her flat's windows) watching the world and his brother go past. The woman resident left her home and discreetly began following Newell along the street.

As luck would have it, the concerned citizen met with her sister and quickly explained to her what she had seen. Both then began to follow Newell and her daughter as they pushed the cart along Duke Street. The two women watched and loitered as Newell pulled the cart into an access lane next to 630 Duke Street. They had the presence of mind to separate and while one of them watched the tenement building, the other went off to fetch the police. Robert Foot, a resident from 636 Duke Street, then came out of a local newsagent's shop, carrying his morning newspaper, totally unaware of the events that were unfolding. As he walked towards his home, one of the women shouted to him, 'There is a woman away up that entry and she is carrying a dead body.' Meanwhile, Newell had reached the head of the lane and found herself in one of a number of backcourts of a block of tenement flats. Worse still, from her point of view, was that the only exit appeared to be the way she had entered, unless she was prepared to climb over a six-foot wall that separated one backcourt from another. Newell, who had been aware of the interest in her presence since the incident at the lorry, panicked. She saw Foot walking up the lane and immediately let go of the little cart, leaving Janet to fend for herself as she began climbing the dividing stone wall.

However, a passing police officer, Constable Thomas McGennet, had also been alerted and appeared in the backcourt. He arrived just in time to find Newell halfway over the wall. 'Where are you going?' he asked Newell. She answered, 'I am going this way.' McGennet took hold of her and pulled her from off the wall. 'I think you had better come this other way,' was his response as he placed her under arrest. Word had spread like wildfire about the commotion behind 630 Duke Street and soon the area was a heaving mass of residents, curious onlookers and downright nosy gossips. Police reinforcement's had arrived but even they had problems trying to keep the curious spectators from encroaching too close. As Newell was led away, she cried out for her daughter, Janet, who had been completely forgotten about during the entire episode. A woman in the crowd stepped out, with Janet holding her hand. A policeman ushered the child away through the hushed throng of spectators. Those same spectators hung their heads in a show of respect as the body of little John Johnston was carried out by two constables.

Newell was taken to the Eastern Police Station in Tobago Street where she was interviewed about that day's incident. She was quite open with the detectives, telling them that her husband John had killed the young boy and then left the house, leaving her with the problem of how to dispose of the body. Young Janet was also questioned and gave a similar story, having been primed by her mother regarding what to say if it ever came to it.

A postmortem was held at the city mortuary, conducted by Professor John Glaister, assisted by Dr John Anderson, pathologist at the city's Victoria Infirmary. Their findings were simply that the young newsvendor had been strangled. Somewhat strangely, the pathologists noted that there had been recent burning to the young lad's scalp and sides of his head. Indeed, both his ears had been completely burned off. No one was really sure if those injuries had been caused accidentally or whether there had been an attempt to destroy some evidence.

The full machinations of the law were put into place in order to locate John Newell. Houses in Coatbridge and in his home village were visited and searched. Descriptions of Newell were passed to the newspapers, whose editors were happy to print the story on their front pages. About nine am on Friday 22nd June, John Newell walked into the police station at Haddington, West Lothian and laid out a copy of that day's newspaper on the desk. He pointed to the front-page story of the discovery of the murder and told the police officer on duty that he was the man they were searching for. Without saying another word, Newell found himself under arrest and in a cell. Yet again, the power of the media had helped in a criminal case.

Enquiries were made locally and it was discovered that Newell had arrived at a Haddington guesthouse the previous day (Thursday) about seven pm. He took a room and told the landlady that he was seeking work on any of the local farms. As John Newell was being detained, his wife stood in the dock at the Eastern Police Court, which was attached to the police office. The courtroom was mobbed with spectators, who filled every seat and stood in every corner. They were totally silent as Bailie John Smith remanded Susan Newell in custody and sent her to Duke Street Prison. It was reported at the time that Newell said nothing during her appearance but that her lips were constantly twitching.

John Newell was later transferred to Glasgow, where he also appeared in court charged with murder and he too was remanded in custody until his trial date. Both Susan and John Newell went on trial at Glasgow High Court at the start of September 1923. The judge, Lord Alness, presided over a jury of eight men and seven women. A plea of insanity at the time of the offence was put forward on Susan's behalf while her husband claimed a special defence of alibi. The two accused sat together in the dock but not once were they seen to exchange even a glance at each other. Once again, the courtroom was packed as the prosecution opened their case.

Witness after witness was called to give evidence. Mrs Young, the Coatbridge landlady, told of letting young Johnston into the house and seeing him enter the Newell's flat. She never saw him leave but assumed that he did. Dickson the lorry driver, gave his evidence without fuss, as did the other witnesses who had observed Newell and her daughter with the go-cart in the various streets. The star witness in the case turned out to be Janet MacLeod, Susan's eight-year-old daughter. She told a hushed court of how she entered the flat in Coatbridge to see the dead body of the boy sprawled on the couch, her mother leaning over it. She detailed how she helped wrap the body in the brightly coloured blanket and how her mother constantly reminded her of what to tell the police should they be caught, which was that her stepfather John had killed the boy.

The next startling event in the trial was the dismissal of the charges against John Newell. His defence counsel was able to show that he was not at home at all on the evening of the murder and witnesses were called to prove this fact. Lord Alness released him from the dock with a stinging rebuke to the prosecution. The judge was of the opinion that, with a minimum of investigation, charges would not have been laid against John Newell nor would he have been brought to trial. Without looking at his wife, Newell stepped down from the dock to freedom.

The trial against Susan continued. Her defence counsel attempted to introduce evidence that showed that she was insane. This was rebutted by Professor Glaister, who had interviewed and examined her while she had been held in custody at the prison. Her counsel then attempted to show that the killing of John Johnston was a spur-of-the-moment act and not a premeditated one. There was also great play made of the point that the prosecution could not provide a motive for the murder. The court had already heard from witnesses that Johnston had no more than 9d (4p) on him at the time of calling at the Newell's. However, as has been seen before, it is not necessary for the prosecution to show motive in order to prove that murder was committed.

The jury adjourned from the courtroom to deliberate its verdict. It took them 37 minutes to return with a verdict of guilty, albeit by a majority. They were, however, unanimous in their recommendation that the prisoner be shown mercy. Lord Alness had no option in the matter. Susan Newell had been convicted of murder, a capital offence, and one for which there was only one punishment – death. Susan Newell showed no emotion as she was led from the dock and taken back to Duke Street Prison to await execution.

Once again, Susan Newell was examined by doctors who declared that she was sane and fit to face sentence. An appeal against that sentence was launched and received considerable support from all quarters. Unfortunately for Susan, politics took a hand in matters. For over 50 years, no woman had been hanged in Scotland. Nine months earlier, in England, 28-year-old Edith Thompson was executed for the murder of her husband. Her hanging caused a public outcry, as there was a widely held belief that she was innocent, the main culprit being her lover and co-accused Frederick Bywaters. Her appeal and those of the public were ignored and she went to her death at the same time and on the same date as Bywaters. Even after that, controversy surrounded her execution, when it turned into a particularly messy affair and it is said, left her executioner John Ellis with nightmares.

The legal authorities in Scotland were keen to remain in symmetry with their counterparts in England. Newell's appeal was refused and she was heard to cry out loud in her cell when told the news by the then Lord Provost of Glasgow. As she was being comforted, she passed out. John Ellis was engaged to carry out the sentence. Just before eight am on 10th October 1923, he entered the condemned cell and quickly pinioned the arms of Susan Newell by fitting a belt around her waist, which held straps designed to tie her elbows to her body. However, in his haste, he failed to securely fasten the straps around her wrists.

As she stepped onto the trapdoor of the gallows, assistant executioner Robert Baxter strapped her legs and thighs, while Ellis placed the noose around her neck and tightened it. Susan wriggled one of her hands free and quickly pulled the white hood from off her head. She threw the hood in Ellis direction and said, 'Don't put that thing over me.'

Fearing another nightmarish incident, Ellis quickly pulled the lever, opening the trapdoor. Susan Newell fell to her death, her unsecured arm flailing wildly and her eyes wide open, staring at the assembled officials who surrounded the gallows, there in the capacity as witnesses to the execution. Ellis later wrote that Susan Newell was not only the calmest person he had ever executed but also the bravest.

As a result of the executions of both Newell and Thompson, Ellis resigned from his job as the country's executioner-in-chief. He turned to alcohol to blot out his memories of horrendous events he had been part of. Within ten months of Newell's execution he attempted to commit suicide by blowing his brains out with a pistol, but failed. He remained a shadow of his former self and eventually, he did kill himself, cutting his throat with an open razor in full view of family members.

Susan Newell never once admitted her guilt and there have been numerous thoughts expressed about the case in various books and articles. What is undeniable is that Susan's husband had walked out on her, she was faced with losing her lodgings, she had been drinking and she lost her temper with John Johnston, possibly over some innocent remark that was made. Enough reasons to argue that she was not thinking straight at the time of the murder. However, it was not enough to infer that she was insane. One thing is absolutely certain: John Johnston was a victim – and so was Susan Newell.

She was the last woman hanged in Scotland.

Chapter 7
Maryhill, May 1924

It is said that in 95% of the cases where children are the victims of murder, the killers are either family members, neighbours, or at the least, acquaintances. This case certainly falls into that category. Charles Boyle was 22 years old and resided with his mother, father and younger sister in their one-roomed flat at 3 Springfield Place, a small cul-de-sac just off Garscube Road in the Maryhill district of Glasgow. The house was basically an infamous 'single end'. This particular area of the city was also considered to be one where only lower working-class families resided. Boyle had suffered from infantile paralysis since a very early age. The effect of this was that his left leg was useless and he required the use of a crutch to get around but he hadn't let his disability hamper him too much and he was able to find spells of employment as a cobbler.

Boyle did not usually reside with his parents, Margaret and Charles, but was doing so because he had just been released from Stobhill Hospital after undergoing surgery to have his left foot amputated at the ankle. The operation had taken place a number of weeks beforehand, so when he was discharged on the morning of Saturday 31st May 1924, he was, in medical terms, as well as could be expected.

By the time Boyle turned up at his new lodgings, it was Saturday afternoon and his first priority was to place bets on a number of horse races with the local bookmaker. He didn't have enough money for all of the bets that he wanted to put on, so he borrowed five shillings from a relative and disappeared for the remainder of the afternoon.

On his return to the house, Boyle was smelling strongly of alcohol. Nonetheless, he invited his father to join him for a drink at a local pub and they left the house together about 4.30pm to go on a pub crawl round some local hostelries. Between pubs, Boyle visited the offices of the bookmaker and collected his winnings. About eight pm that night, father and son tried to buy drinks in two other pubs but were refused service because they were too drunk. It was at this point, they parted company and Boyle (senior) decided to go home.

When he arrived there, his wife was waiting for him. Almost immediately a fierce argument broke out between them. Susan Boyle was livid that her husband had come home in a drunken condition, especially as she hadn't been invited on the pub crawl and also because her son hadn't seen fit to give her some of his winnings from the bookmaker in lieu of housekeeping money. At this juncture, Boyle obviously threatened or offered some violence to his wife, for she ran out of the house and disappeared into the night. Fearing she had gone to get the police to him, he put his jacket on and left the house. As he made his way down the common stairs, he met his wife who was on her way back up. She was alone. As she began arguing with him again, Boyle fled the close mouth, his wife's tirade ringing in his ears. He intended to go and spend the night with a work colleague who resided nearby. When the facts are considered, this was a wise move by Boyle. He had an appallingly bad habit of violence towards his wife and had served an ever-increasing number of prison sentences for his violent behaviour towards her. His last period of imprisonment – 15 months – had ended only four weeks previously.

Boyle (junior) arrived back home about 10pm. He was so drunk that, in combination with his missing limb, he had difficulty in climbing the one flight of stairs that led to his mother's flat. In the interval between father leaving and son arriving home, Susan Boyle had partaken of some alcohol. Not enough to make her drunk but a sufficient amount to make her more argumentative than ever. Even when her son tried to give her some money by way of housekeeping, she continued to berate him. Charles Boyle refused to take any more of his mother's verbal abuse and silenced her, for all time, by slashing her throat with an open razor. Blood spouted like a fountain from the huge wound and he let her fall forward – she was dead before she hit the floor. Blood soaked the mat on which she lay, lifeless and face down.

The killing, horrible as it was, didn't stop there. Two small children belonging to an upstairs neighbour, were later found in the Boyle house with their throats cut too. William Devlin, a five-year-old, was found lying across the hearth of the fireplace (fortunately, the fire had not been lit), and initial reports suggested that his head had almost been severed from the rest of his body. May Devlin, his three-year-old sister, was lying next to Mrs Boyle's body. But why should they have been in the Boyle house? It is known that they were in the habit of playing in and around the close and on the stairs on an almost daily basis. Both children had been seen earlier, playing in the backcourt at the same time as eating pieces of bread. How they had got in the house, no one is quite sure. Were they visiting with Mrs Boyle when her son came home? Or were they dragged in later, after Mrs Boyle had been done to death, maybe because they had witnessed something that they shouldn't have?

Charles Boyle, calmly and without much fuss or noise, gathered up his crutch, put on his jacket and left the house. He took time to lock the front door behind him and hobbled off down the stairs. He stopped momentarily to wash his hands of the blood and wipe his crutch with a cloth at the stairhead washbasin, all of which was observed by a neighbour.

It wasn't until just after 10.45pm that the ghastly scene in the Boyle household was discovered. Eleven-year-old Sarah Boyle, the youngest daughter, arrived home from an evening out at the cinema with a friend. She had actually arrived home earlier in the evening, just after 10pm, and had seen her brother Charles washing his hands at the tap in the close but did not approach him. She freely admitted later that she was scared of her brother because of the aggressive attitude he constantly showed towards their mother. She went off to visit her friends but returned almost an hour later.

She found the house locked and as there was no answer to her persistent knocking, she called at the home of a neighbour, where she was given a spare key to her flat. Sarah entered it and immediately discovered the macabre scene. She screamed. Neighbours rushed to her aid and were confronted with the grim sight of three dead bodies and blood-soaked floor coverings and furniture. One neighbour was sent the short distance to Camperdown Police Station and informed the officers on duty there of what had been discovered. They attended immediately at the house in great numbers. The first thing they did was force back the large groups of onlookers who had already gathered as word had spread quickly throughout the district.

Another nameless neighbour had the presence of mind to send a message to Charles Boyle (senior) at his workmate's home, telling him to return immediately. He did so, and on his arrival, was arrested before he had even reached the close mouth. He was released almost as quickly, when his story checked out and other developments took place. Detectives were summoned to the scene and immediately began investigations. During a cursory search of the house, a bloodstained open razor was found lying on the floor behind the front door. Rather oddly, when police asked for medical experts to attend the scene, all they got was a police casualty surgeon, who would only confirm death in each of the three cases. Instructions were then received from the Procurator-Fiscal's office that the bodies should remain in situ overnight as a full forensic examination would take place the following morning in the cold light of day. A police guard was mounted all night on the close entry at Springfield Place.

In the midst of all this police activity, Charles Boyle (junior) sprang a surprise on the police. He walked into Camperdown Police Station and surrendered himself to the sergeant behind the desk. He was temporarily detained while senior officers debated the best way to proceed. A number of senior police officers noted that Boyle, at the time of his arrest, was not smelling strongly of alcohol. Dr Lipsey, acting casualty surgeon, who was already present at the police station, having just come from the murder scene, examined Boyle at great length. His assessment was that Boyle understood what was happening and that he was fit enough to be charged and detained, which would add some credence to the suggestion of Boyle's sobriety. The police lost no time in charging Boyle with the three murders. He stood quietly as the accusations were levelled at him. When the police officer finished reading over the charges, Boyle said in reply, 'I done it. I did it purposely to get myself the rope. I had not the courage to do myself in and I wanted someone to do it for me. You can tell that to Lord Alness or somebody.'

It did not take long for Boyle to be brought to trial. Just four weeks later, on Monday 30th June 1924, Boyle entered the dock of the High Court of Glasgow. Lord Ormidale presided over the events and after a jury was sworn in, a special plea of insanity was entered on Boyle's behalf. Almost immediately, witness after witness, mainly neighbours from Springfield Place, took up position in the witness box and detailed a catalogue of incidents over the years involving drink-sodden arguments, fights and disturbances, all of them emanating from the Boyle household and all of them involving a combination of mother, father and son. Some incidents involved all three and cries of 'murder, murder' were a common occurrence too.

Medical evidence was then brought to bear and this took over the remainder of the trial. First up was Professor John Glaister Jnr. He spoke of having carried out the postmortem examinations on each of the three bodies. Both children died as a result of loss of blood due to having their throats cut by a razor or other similar sharp instrument. There were no other injuries on either of their bodies. In Mrs Boyle's case, death was due to the same cause as the children – loss of blood caused by a gaping throat wound. However, in the professor's opinion, Mrs Boyle fought for her life. She had numerous wounds on her arms and hands, suggesting that she tried to defend herself from the murderous attack. He was also at a loss to suggest a motive for any of the murders. Glaister was next asked about his opinion on the state of mind of the accused man. He told the court that his belief was that 'anything abnormal in Boyle or his conduct on that day (of the murders) was due to alcohol.' Thereafter, the Crown case was concluded.

The defence case began with a number of witnesses giving evidence that they had been in the vicinity of the murder scene on the night in question and had either seen or heard nothing out of the ordinary. Then, Dr James MacDonald, medical superintendent of Hawkhead Mental Hospital in Renfrewshire was called to give his opinion of matters. He stated that he had examined Boyle only a week before the trial and could not find any traces of insanity. However, taking Boyle's past medical history into consideration, where he had attempted suicide twice previously, once by drinking ammonia and the other by throwing himself into the local canal, MacDonald's judgement was that Boyle suffered from psychic epilepsy. In a case of ordinary epilepsy, there is usually a physical seizure which can be observed. With psychic epilepsy, the disturbance is unseen and occurs in the mind. MacDonald stated that Boyle's memory of the events was almost blank and his only recollections of that terrible day were of drinking in the pub in the afternoon and then being charged by police in the middle of the night.

MacDonald stated that because of this, his opinion that Boyle's mental condition on the night of the murders was such that if he did what he was accused of, then he did not know what he was doing and therefore he could not be held responsible for his actions. He further added that if he had been allowed to see Boyle on that particular night, in all probability he would have certified him insane. In answer to questions from the advocate-depute, MacDonald emphasised that the murder of the two children was itself the act of an insane person. No amount of alcohol alone could have led to this crime being committed. The first day of the trial ended on this point and immediately at the beginning of the second day, intimation was made to the judge that, as a result of the evidence heard the day before, Charles Boyle now wished to offer a guilty plea, not to the murders, but to reduced charges of culpable homicide.

Boyle had sat throughout the trial with his head bowed, paying hardly any attention to what was going on around him. He occasionally moved his crutch from one position to another in the dock, as he sat cross-legged, causing the trouser leg of his missing limb to flop lifelessly. When asked by Lord Ormidale if his change of plea was true, Boyle replied in a very gruff voice, 'Yes, I plead guilty.'

The advocate-depute addressed the court and declared that he was prepared to accept the reduced pleas. He pointed out that the pleas now offered proved two main points. First, that Boyle, and no one else, had killed Mrs Boyle and the two children and second, that the defence had failed to prove their special defence of insanity. By pleading in those terms, they were establishing that Boyle was a sane man at the time the crimes were committed. However, Boyle's past history and the medical opinion heard in the case, suggested that he was suffering from some form of aberration of mind or mental unsoundness.

Lord Ormidale also intimated that he fully agreed that Boyle was not insane but suffering from some form of mental abnormality. The judge reminded those in the courtroom that Boyle was greatly intoxicated at the time the savagery was committed but that this was no excuse and, in the eyes of the law, did not diminish the accused's responsibility. He then went on to remind those present that Boyle had been a frequent visitor to the docks of various courts. From 1919, Boyle had been charged with assaults and other serious offences on a regular basis and this showed him to be a man of violent passion and temper. The judge was also extremely critical of the authorities, in particular those in charge of Stoneyetts Mental Institute. Boyle had been incarcerated there after one of his suicide attempts. However, he escaped from his detention and the authorities made no attempt to recapture him.

Boyle was ordered to stand up to hear his sentence. Lord Ormidale said he believed Boyle to be a very violent criminal and, as a consequence, considered sending him to prison for life. However, looking at all the facts of the case, he was now prepared to limit his sentence to one of 15 years penal servitude, with the proviso that the authorities would regularly monitor his mental health.

After hearing his sentence, Boyle turned and slowly hobbled down the stairs to the cells below. Loud cheers and applause from the public benches in the courtroom accompanied him all the way.

Chapter 8

Port Dundas, May 1925

Gangs have been part of Glasgow's culture for three centuries now. From the 1870's 'Penny Mob' until the present day, (the most recent reports suggest that we have almost 170 gangs in the city), they have festered in the slums and later, the housing estates. 'Fleet', 'Tongs' and 'Gringos' were among the more popular names for the gangs. Even 'Cowboys' and 'Indians' were used as labels for groups of thugs. During World War 1, when many men were away doing other duties, the Indians' membership was predominantly female. Nonetheless, they were one of the largest gangs and had, at various times, over 1,000 'members'.

The gangs collected money from various sources, mainly by running protection rackets. It was claimed that any levies raised would be used to pay for the court fines of those members unlucky enough to have fallen foul of the law. One gang specialised in 'protecting' dance halls while many others 'looked after' local shops and delivery vans. One such gang, the 'Port Dundas Tongs' operated in the area the name suggests. The district, just a stone's throw from the city centre area, hasn't always been what it is today – an area full of small industrial estates that contain businesses of all sizes. In the 1920's, the neighbourhood was one of street after street of tenement houses, occupied, as one newspaper put it, by those people of the working class or lower. Overcrowding appeared to be the norm, with the large majority of families living in one roomed accommodation and the district had a notorious reputation as a breeding ground for criminals of all levels.

One Saturday evening in May 1925, a 27-year-old Indian pedlar found himself in Port Dundas, in the wrong house at the wrong time; a mistake that would ultimately cost him his life. Noorh Mohammed was a native of the Punjab in India and had been invited to come to Scotland in late 1924 by some friends, who were already here and working as door-to-door hosiery salesmen. They sold all types of fabrics, from men's handkerchiefs and ladies' silk scarves to curtains and carpets, all from a suitcase. While they resided in Glasgow, they travelled extensively all over the west of Scotland. It has to be said that Glasgow then had a larger than average quota of ethnic minorities.

Most had settled here after having fought in World War 1 and sent for families, relatives and friends to join them.

On the evening of Saturday 16th May, Mohammed returned from an all-day trip to Kilmarnock, where he had been hawking his wares. He called at a house at 5 Clyde Street in Port Dundas, that of his friend Nathoo Mohamed and his wife, Louie. While in this house, three men – John Keen, John McCormick and William Dayer – came to the door and spoke with Nathoo in the hallway of his home. Only two of the men entered, the third – Dayer – stood, as if on guard, at the open front door. The story that circulated later was that the visitors produced two daggers and asked Nathoo if he would buy them. When Nathoo refused to purchase the weapons, an argument developed, into which Noorh became embroiled. From all accounts, Noorh's involvement became more intense and threats and counter-threats were issued. At one point during the confrontation, Nathoo Mohamed became so frightened that he ran out of the house and up the street, dressed only in a billowing bed sheet, and sought refuge in a tenement at 56 Water Street, which just happened to be the home of Noorh Mohammed.

After a few more minutes, the men left the flat without any further trouble. As they loitered about in the street outside, they observed Noorh Mohammed leaving the close mouth and making his way along Clyde Street towards his home. As they were to claim later, the men followed him because they were afraid that he was heading for the local police office to inform on them. This was a strange claim to make considering that Mohammed was going in the opposite direction from the local police station. Nonetheless, it must have been a relief to them to see Noorh enter the close at 56 Water Street. He climbed the five flights of stairs to the top floor two-bedroomed flat that he shared with five other of his countrymen and met up with Nathoo, who was already there relating his story to his friends.

Keen, McCormick and Dayer wasted no time in alerting their friends and before too long, a crowd of almost 100 had gathered in the street outside 56 Water Street. It has to be said that the vast majority of the mob could be described as only 'interested onlookers'. They knew that a fight was about to take place and they all wanted to see it. This didn't help the Indians in the house upstairs as they witnessed the build up of the mass of locals, in and around the close, and they quickly became panic-stricken. Before long, the unruly gang climbed the stairs and began hammering on the front door of the Indian's flat. They were demanding that Nathoo Mohamed come out to face them, which he did, but he also took a broom with him, which allowed him to keep those at the front of the crowd at arms length.

This only enraged the mob further and Nathoo took a beating. He was punched and kicked and then someone in the crowd threw a large stone which hit Nathoo on the chest, seriously injuring him. He fell backwards into the open doorway of the flat, as his friends dragged him further into the hallway before slamming the door shut. The crowd began battering on the door again until it was opened, and this time Noorh Mohammed appeared in the doorway armed with the same broom. Very quickly, he was overpowered by Robert Fletcher, who had grabbed his arm. As he struggled and stretched to free himself, John Keen produced one of the daggers and stabbed Noorh twice in the chest. His resistance overcome, he was then dragged by Keen, Fletcher, McCormick and others, across the landing and down two flights of stairs, under the feet of the crowd, some of whom took the opportunity to kick the injured man on the way.

Back on the top landing, the remainder of the mob had crowded through the open front door and began to attack the inhabitants, who had all gathered together in the kitchen. Cups, saucers, furniture and even pieces of coal from the bunker, were all thrown at the Indians as they huddled together. After only a few minutes of this frenzied activity, the house and its contents were totally wrecked. Very quickly, the battling mob dispersed, as if given some silent command; more likely they were warned by lookouts that the police had been contacted and were now making their way to the scene. With the tenement stairs now deserted and although injured, Nathoo Mohamed went looking for his friend Noorh and quickly found him on the landing two floors below. Noorh was barely conscious and saturated in blood. Nathoo carried his friend back upstairs and put him to bed.

Just as they were about to send out for a doctor, police arrived at the door. On seeing how badly Noorh was injured, police called for an ambulance immediately and he was taken to the city's Royal Infirmary where he was examined and found to be suffering from two deep stab wounds to the left side of his upper chest. Arteries had been severed and he was bleeding profusely. Sadly, as he was being rushed to the operating theatre, Noorh succumbed to his wounds.

Police swarmed all over Water Street and the surrounding area as the news of Noorh's murder spread. The home of the Indian pedlars had not only been destroyed but during the fracas and confusion, their sale goods had been stolen too. From the houses of many 'witnesses', various items of stolen property were recovered including scarves and pullovers. Statements were obtained from those persons who were both willing and unwilling to give them. During the early hours of Sunday morning, the police had made so much progress in the inquiry they were able to identify and apprehend those they thought were the ringleaders in the murder of Noorh Mohammed. Seven men and one woman were arrested in swoops on various houses in the district. At one house, during a search, a dagger which had been broken into three pieces, was recovered and retained by police.

Later that Sunday, about noon, John Keen walked into the local police station and gave himself up. One other male was apprehended later the same night, and altogether, nine men and one woman (John Keen's wife) appeared in court on the Monday morning. All were charged with murder, assault and theft. Three of the accused, Keen, Fletcher and McCormick were further charged with assault on Nathoo Mohamed. All accused were remanded in custody.

As the police probe deepened, so it became more apparent who had played what part in the events of Saturday night. By the evening of Monday, six of the accused, including Mrs Keen, were released, all charges against them having been dropped. Only Keen, Fletcher, McCormick and Thomas Andrew remained in custody.

As all these locals were appearing in court on Monday, other residents were attending Noorh Mohammed's funeral. A short service took place in the mortuary of the Royal Infirmary and then the cortege left for the journey to Riddrie Cemetery. About 50 of Noorh's countrymen walked slowly behind the hearse all the way to the cemetery, where crowds of people, mainly women and numbering in excess of 500, were waiting at the gates and at the open graveside. In keeping with Noorh's religious faith, the lid was removed from his coffin and all the mourners filed past in silence. At the end of the interment, only his countrymen remained at the open grave and began to feast on fruits such as oranges, bananas and dates.

In the time between the detentions of those thought responsible and the opening of the trial, one of the four men – Thomas Andrew – was released. Another man, William Dayer, who was one of the ten originally detained, was re-arrested and detained. Dayer faced a charge of involvement in the assault on Nathoo Mohamed at the Clyde Street house. And so, on Tuesday 1st September 1925, four young men – John Keen, John McCormick, Robert Fletcher and William Dayer – went on trial in the North Court of the High Court of Justiciary in Glasgow, presided over by Lord Ormidale. The courtroom was packed to capacity, mainly with locals from the Port Dundas district. Quite a number of other persons were turned away from the courthouse as it was full. A jury of nine women and six men were sworn in and heard the charges being read out against all the accused. Keen, McCormick and Dayer were charged with assaulting and intimidating Nathoo Mohamed in his home at 5 Clyde Street and 'threatening to stab him unless he produced jumpers and scarves to them'. Keen, McCormick and Fletcher were further charged with murdering Noorh Mohammed by 'seizing hold of him, kicking him, beating him and stabbing him with a dagger.' The third charge referred to assault and the stealing of property.

The Crown case was simply that the four accused, as part of the gang called 'Port Dundas Tongs', were trying to extort money or goods from the Indian pedlars in exchange for not harming them. When the money or goods failed to be handed over, the Indians were threatened with violence, culminating in the murder of one of their number. One of the first witnesses to give evidence was Robert Purdon, a 21-year-old gang member from Crawford Street, Port Dundas, who told a hushed court that Keen had handed him a dagger in the street outside 56 Water Street after the fight had taken place. As the crowd disappeared off the street and into other closes, someone said to him, 'Give it to McCall. He'll throw it in the canal.' Purdon did as he was instructed and gave the dagger to fellow gang member Joseph McCall, a 24-year-old from Mid Wharf Street, who was the next witness called. McCall told the court that far from throwing the dagger in the canal, he decided to keep the weapon, but did not want to take it home with him, so he went to an empty building near to his home and found a hiding place for the knife in the chimney-breast of the building.

In the aftermath of the murder, James Purdon, an older brother of Robert Purdon, got to hear of his brother's involvement in the affair. He then called on McCall and impressed upon him of the need to return the dagger. McCall told Purdon where he had hidden the weapon, allowing him to recover it and hand it over to the detectives involved in the case. The dagger was produced in court as the murder weapon. This crucial evidence for the Crown showed the unbroken chain of possession from Purdon through McCall and all the way back to the hands of Keen.

Professor John Glaister Snr was also a major prosecution witness. His evidence was that he examined a number of stains found on John Keen's clothes and on the dagger allegedly in his possession and came to the opinion that all the stains were of human blood. Glaister also examined the broken dagger found during the house searches but could find no trace of blood on any of the three parts. Glaister also performed the postmortem examination on Mohammed's body. He found that the cause of death had been due to two stab wounds to the chest, one of which had pierced the salesman's heart and cut an artery causing Mohammed to bleed to death.

During the first day of the trial, no evidence was led against William Dayer, and as a consequence, all charges against him were withdrawn and he was freed from the dock and allowed to go. The five remaining Indians all gave evidence as to what they had seen. Most gave details of having to pay a 'fee', money or other valuables, to the gang members so that they could go about the area without being molested.

Over the next four days, other witnesses, both for the prosecution and the defence, came and told their stories to a packed courtroom. Then it was time for the summing up of all counsel and the judge's final charge to the jury. During the course of these speeches, it was noted that both Fletcher and McCormick appeared quite relaxed while Keen wept openly into a handkerchief. The jury retired to consider their verdicts at 3.50pm After debating the matter for an hour and 35 minutes, they returned to the courtroom and the foreman read out the decision of the jury. They had found that Keen and McCormick were guilty of assaulting and intimidating Nathoo Mohamed, while Keen alone was guilty, by a unanimous verdict, of murdering Noorh Mohammed. Even although it was a unanimous verdict, the jury still asked that a recommendation for mercy be considered in this case. Fletcher was found guilty of Noorh's culpable homicide. On the third charge, of assaulting the other occupants of 56 Water Street and stealing all their goods, both Keen and Fletcher were found 'not proven'.

On hearing the verdicts, the accused mens' heads dropped as they sat back down in the dock. McCormick was the first to be sentenced. He showed no expression or emotion as he received nine months imprisonment for his part in the assault on Mohamed. Next up came Keen. The judge's words rang round the hushed court as the black cap was placed on his head and he sentenced the 28-year-old to death. The execution was scheduled to take place on 24th September. Keen sat down slowly as Fletcher stood up to hear his sentence of seven years penal servitude for culpable homicide. Fletcher did not get to sit down. Almost on the last word of the judge's sentencing, the other two prisoners were ushered to their feet by the police officers who sat beside them. As they stood and turned to go down the stairs to the cells below, Keen turned back to the court and said to Lord Ormidale, 'Can I ask you a question?'

The judge agreed to Keen's request and asked what his question was. Keen then stated, 'Your Lordship, I don't think there has been much justice in this case at all. If I had gone into the witness box I would have cleared myself.' Keen was looking around the court, almost as if he was appealing for someone to agree with him. Seeing that no support was forthcoming, Keen continued, 'I shall leave behind me a full written statement which will make it hot for one other man. Why were witnesses dropped who would have spoken on certain things had they been called, such as the other dagger? Instead, I was picked up alone. Why should I be the only one to suffer? I thought there was justice in the High Court, but now I know there is none. I have been called a hooligan and a gangster, but this I never was.'

The judge, clearly taken aback by Keen's statement, or outburst, whichever way you view it, replied, 'I'm afraid that what you have said has not been to your advantage. If you have any representations to make, you had better consult with your law agent and he will advise you on the matter quite considerably and sympathetically.' But Keen wasn't listening any more. He was shouting at those who would listen to him and blurted out, 'I asked for the privilege to go into the witness box this morning'.

Lord Ormidale, by now no longer wishing to discuss the matter further in open court, boomed out from the bench, 'I think you had better go,' dismissing him with a hand gesture to the attending police officers. These officers took their cue from that and began ushering Keen down the stairs again. As they all disappeared from the court's view, Keen could be heard sobbing loudly. Someone from the public galleries shouted, 'Cheer up, John,' but was quickly quietened by police officers stationed there.

John Keen went to jail. The recommendation for mercy was forwarded to the appropriate authorities but was immediately rejected. Keen had no right to appeal his conviction for that law did not come into force until October the following year (See chapter 9).

On the fine sunny morning of 24th September 1925, John Keen walked the 22 steps from the condemned cell to the scaffold in Duke Street Prison in Glasgow.

As a final postscript, Keen's execution was the first to be witnessed, in an official capacity, by a woman, Bailie Mary Bell. Interviewed afterwards, she said that the entire experience had been 'quiet, solemn and impressive.' Previously, she had held the view that capital punishment, in certain murder cases, was necessary, and after viewing this execution, she was still of that opinion.

Chapter 9

River Clyde, October 1927

On the morning of Saturday 15th October 1927, bright autumnal sunshine reflected on the surface of the River Clyde as George Geddes, river warden of the Royal Humane Society, was out in his rowing boat. He was towing a floating platform up the river to the Polmadie Bridge, where it would be used by joiners, who were carrying out repairs. The water level of the river had been controlled by use of weirs to assist the joiners in their work. The river was at least 18 inches lower than usual and it was this fact that brought one of the most horrific cases of murder to the notice of the police and the public of Glasgow.

As Geddes pulled gently on his oars, his attention was attracted to a white parcel lying on a mud bank on the north side of the river. Instinctively, he steered towards it and hauled it into his small boat by the rope which bound the package. Curious to find out what he had recovered, Geddes cut the rope and the bundle unravelled itself as a human head rolled out into the bottom of the boat. Although Geddes was very used to dealing with death (his job entailed the recovery of all corpses from the river environs), he was still shocked by his discovery. Looking further into the parcel, he found that it also contained two legs and an arm.

The police were summoned and took the remains to the Central Police Station mortuary. There, they were examined for any clues as to the identity of the deceased. None were forthcoming and the police knew that they would have great difficulty in solving this mystery of two parts – who was the victim and who was the murderer?

The parcel contained two legs severed just below the knees, one thigh and a left arm and hand. The ring finger of the hand had been hacked off but was later found wrapped in paper elsewhere in the parcel. The head had been severely mutilated in an attempt to avoid any identification. The forehead had five or six large gashes across it, both cheeks were slashed open, the nose had been cut off completely and half the tongue was missing. The head and face had also been blackened by burning.

All police officers in Glasgow were recalled to duty that Saturday afternoon to assist in searches which were ongoing along both banks of the river and in all buildings bordering these areas. The object of the police search was to find the torso of the mutilated body. Professor John Glaister was called to the police mortuary and asked to assist police with a postmortem examination. He was quickly able to tell them that the victim was 'a well-nourished woman who was past middle age, probably in her sixties.' All missing persons files were checked but no matches found. The help of newspapers was enlisted and the story of the grisly find released to them, along with an urgent request for public help in identifying the victim.

All Sunday morning, a queue of people, who wanted to report possible missing persons, formed up outside the Central Police Station. Relatives, friends and neighbours waited patiently to tell of their suspicions but only a few people got past the initial interview stage and were allowed to view the grisly remains. One such helpful witness identified the corpse and police went off to investigate. They were somewhat surprised to find their named 'victim' answering the door of her house to them when they called! However, late on Sunday afternoon, a woman called at the police office and told detectives that she had just returned from working in Rothesay but when she had called at her mother-in-law's home, she found it unoccupied and clear of furniture. She was taken to the mortuary where she positively identified the disfigured head as that of her relative.

Two detectives, one of them Det Lt Stirton (see also chapter 4), were despatched to the home of Mrs Agnes Arbuckle at 213 Main Street, Gorbals but when they got there, there was no answer to their repeated knocking on the door. The officers left the scene and made their way to 241 Thistle Street which was nearby. This was the home of James McKay, son of Agnes Arbuckle and husband of the woman who had given all this latest information to the police.* McKay was interviewed by the detectives and during the discussion about his mother's whereabouts, he blurted, 'She is dead. She died about ten days ago. I put part of her in the Clyde. The rest is in the bunker.' The detectives arrested McKay and thereafter took him to his mother's house at Main Street. Once all three men were inside the front door, McKay pointed to the kitchen coal bunker and said, 'It's in there and the saw is in the room.'

Stirton moved over to the bunker and opened the lid. At first it appeared to be full of coal but after moving a few of the larger lumps, he came across a brown paper parcel. On opening it, he discovered that it contained a

---

* Mrs Arbuckle had been married more than once, but had reverted back to her maiden name after being widowed.

human right arm. At this stage, McKay was taken from the house straight to the Central Police Station, where he was detained. The police quickly returned in greater numbers to Mrs Arbuckle's home and carried out a more thorough search. In the coal bunker, right down at the bottom, two more parcels were found. Each contained a piece of the torso, which appeared to have been severed in half.

James McKay appeared at court in a rather dishevelled state. His hair was uncombed, he looked as if he had slept in his clothes and he was barefooted. He was remanded in custody while the police made further investigations into the case.

Mrs Arbuckle was 60 years of age and had lived in her top-floor, two-roomed flat for 17 years before her demise. Neighbours described her as a quiet woman who had brought up three sons. One of her lads was reported killed in action during World War I, for which she received a weekly pension of nine shillings. Another son died from disease in 1921. James McKay was her youngest boy. But what the police could not fathom out was why a son would murder his mother, then cut up her body and throw it in to the river? From contemporary reports and the transcripts of the subsequent trial, James McKay was 37 years of age, married and resided in the Thistle Street tenement flat with his wife and young son, John. He had fought in World War I, but had been taken prisoner and spent three years in a POW camp. Recently, his married life had not been holding up too well. Money was very tight and his wife had been forced to find employment as a live-in cook at a hotel in Rothesay for the summer season, leaving their child in James's care. James was also employed but was having trouble due to his excessive drinking habits. He was spending all his earnings on alcohol and as a consequence, had fallen far behind with his rent payments for his home.

On 20th September 1927, McKay telephoned his wife, pleading for her to return to the family home. He claimed he was lonely and depressed. He further stated that if she did not return, he would sell up the house. She refused to come home. The next day Mrs Meiklejohn, a neighbour of the McKay's, had called on Mrs Arbuckle to inform her of her son's wild behaviour. He had begun to sell off his household furniture, always appeared to be drunk and was, in Mrs Meiklejohn's words, 'behaving himself funnily'. Mrs Arbuckle visited her son but an argument ensued. After she had left, James McKay called on Mrs Meiklejohn. He was extremely angry and assaulted her in response to her admitting she had informed on him. However, any advice received from his mother had fallen on deaf ears, as by the following day, McKay had sold off every last piece of his furniture.

McKay met up with an old drinking friend, Owen Watters, who resided with his mother at 3 Hospital Street, Gorbals. McKay related to Watters of the predicament he was in, with severe rent arrears and marriage problems. Watters agreed to let McKay and his son share his room in his mother's house. This new domestic situation suited McKay for two reasons. He could go drinking with his friend anytime he wanted and he would also have a ready-made babysitter for his son in his friend's mother, Mrs McArthur.

Police enquiries revealed that Mrs Arbuckle had collected her pension at Gorbals Post Office on 28th September but had not turned up in the weeks after that. No matter to whom the police spoke, no one could remember seeing Mrs Arbuckle after 28th September. However, there was a glut of witnesses willing to provide statements to the authorities regarding McKay's financial circumstances. One minute McKay hadn't a penny in his pockets, the next he would be counting out banknotes in front of astonished onlookers. All this occurred after he had been sacked from his job on 30th September.

McKay let it be known throughout the neighbourhood that his mother was ill and had taken to her bed to recover. At one stage, he told neighbours that his mother had gone on holiday to Rothesay in an attempt to overcome her illness. This very neatly accounted for his constant coming and going from his mother's home, as he was allegedly 'keeping an eye on things' while she was away. Unfortunately for McKay, neighbours noticed that he appeared to be removing furniture from the house, sometimes accompanied by other people and occasionally using a barrow to assist with the bulkier items. When confronted by concerned residents, McKay explained by saying that his mother had returned from Rothesay, was now staying with friends in Blantyre and was considering moving into a one-roomed house to be near them. As a result, she could not take all her furniture with her.

In the first two weeks of October, McKay visited his wife in Rothesay on at least two occasions, spending a couple of days in the resort with her before returning to Glasgow. McKay showed a number of witnesses a bank book in his mother's name which had over £80 deposited in it. He also showed a slip of paper which said, 'Pay the bearer the sum of £40 and oblige Mrs Agnes Arbuckle'. Similar pieces of paper were found on McKay at the time of his arrest along with others where his mother's name and signature appeared numerous times along with the date, 'Glasgow 17th October 1927.' A will, made out in favour of McKay, and the aforementioned bank book were also recovered when McKay was arrested at his home. He had been sitting on them.

Another witness, John Russell, spoke of assisting McKay remove a tin trunk from Mrs Arbuckle's house on 12th October. The trunk was very heavy and they had difficulty carrying it down five flights of stairs. Once in the street, McKay heaved it onto his shoulder and carried it as far as Clelland Street before he stopped to rest. The following day, Russell again helped McKay with the tin trunk, this time in returning it to Mrs Arbuckle's home. McKay paid Russell for his assistance and Russell noted that McKay was in possession of six or seven gold half-sovereign coins.

On Monday 12th December, James McKay went on trial at the High Court in Glasgow, charged with having between 27th September and 15th October, in the house at 213 Main Street, Glasgow, then occupied by the deceased Mrs Agnes Arbuckle, assaulted her, cut her on the face and neck and body with a sharp instrument and murdered her. McKay also faced a further charge of having robbed his mother of a bank book and articles of furniture. McKay pleaded not guilty to both charges and entered a special plea of defence that at the time of the alleged crimes he was insane and in such a state of mental weakness as to make him not responsible for his actions.

The courtroom was littered with large bulky items of furniture, all of which had been lodged as productions in the case. When McKay entered the dock and saw all the various pieces around him, a faint smile crossed his lips. Very quickly, a jury of six women and nine men was empanelled and the case got started. What rapidly became evident as the initial evidence was heard was that McKay sold off all of his household furniture between 20th and 22nd September and then, over the following two to three weeks, paid off his rent arrears and began moving his mother's furniture into his home.

Evidence was also heard from the police of the finding of Mrs Arbuckle's bank book and the pieces of paper with the incriminating writing on them. One officer spoke of having taken plaster casts of shoeprints found in the mud on the banks of the river where the original parcel had been recovered. When McKay was arrested, his shoes were taken from him and compared to the casts. They were identical; hence the reason for McKay appearing barefoot at his first court appearance on 17th October.

Two tin trunks were recovered from the house. One contained fragments of burnt flesh and a copious number of bloodstains, while the other held a number of books. When the books were removed, a pair of corset bones was recovered sticking to the bottom of the trunk. They were stuck because they were saturated in blood.

Professor Glaister went through his evidence methodically and without any hurry. He stated that he was of the opinion that when he examined the remains of Mrs Arbuckle, she had been dead for between ten and 14 days.

Those parts of the body found in the Clyde had only been in the water between 24 and 48 hours, as they hardly differed in decomposition from those parts found in the house. He also suggested that whoever had dismembered the body had been unskilled and, although it had probably only taken about two hours to do it, had absolutely no knowledge of anatomy. Furthermore, the burning of the head and the scorchmarks on the torso had taken place after death had occurred, due to the lack of blistering of the skin. It had obviously been done in an attempt to destroy evidence and, more importantly, avoid identification. The professor's opinion was that the cause of death was due to a loss of blood and shock, occurring from the many severe wounds inflicted on the elderly woman.

MacKay's sanity was then discussed at great length by a number of eminent medical witnesses, who had, at various times during his incarceration, examined him. Their combined opinion was that McKay appeared to be of sound mind and above average intelligence. At times, he appeared depressed and sullen but not one of them could find any evidence of any abnormality or any recent temporary insanity. McKay was, however, an alcoholic.

No witnesses were called for the defence.

The trial went straight to counsel's final speeches and the judge's summing up. The judge, Lord Ormidale, made the point that an accused person is innocent until proved guilty and that is the job of the Crown to prove. However, an accused is also presumed to be sane unless it is proved otherwise and that is a job for the defence to prove. In this particular case, no evidence had been produced to show any mental abnormality on behalf of the prisoner.

The jury deliberated for 26 minutes before returning to the courtroom. They brought in unanimous verdicts of guilty of murder and robbery. As the foreman of the jury announced 'guilty as libelled', several woman in the courtroom, including Mrs McKay, burst into uncontrollable sobbing. McKay stood ramrod straight in the dock as Lord Ormidale sentenced him to death, the execution date being set for 4th January 1928 at Duke Street Prison. McKay showed no trace of emotion and as he turned to make his way down to the cells, someone from the rear of the court shouted, 'Cheer up'.

One strange thread appears to run through this entire case and it is one that has never been satisfactorily explained. James McKay's wife played a major role in the circumstances but was never called to account. On 28th September – the last day anyone can remember seeing Agnes Arbuckle – Mrs McKay called at her home but found her out. A neighbour, Mrs Agnes Torrance, informed her that Mrs Arbuckle was probably away to collect her pension from the Post Office. McKay waited for her mother-in-law's return.

When they did meet up, there is no record of the topic of conversation, but it is well known that Agnes Arbuckle did not get on with her daughter-in-law. At one time Mrs Arbuckle offered her son £1 a week as a separation allowance. All he had to do to qualify for the money was to stay away from his wife.

From Mrs McKay herself, it is learned that the women quarrelled about something, most probably the selling of the family furniture and on her return to Hospital Street she took up the same argument with her husband; this was witnessed by Owen Watters and his mother. As a consequence of all the disharmony, James McKay visited his mother that evening and she was never seen alive again.

After these events Mrs McKay returned to Rothesay on 30th September, the day her husband was sacked from his job. She did not return until 15th October. The evidence points to James McKay having disposed of the parcel of body parts into the river on the night and morning of 13th/14th October. Mrs Meiklejohn said he called at her home about 05.50 am on the morning of 14th and had dirty hands, face and clothes. His shoes were covered in mud and she thought he looked as if he 'had been through a ploughed field'. Was it just down to chance that Mrs McKay returned the day after some of the body parts were dumped?

On the same day she immediately went to her mother-in-law's house and removed a bed from it and took it to her own home at Thistle Street. Yet, the following day when she went to the police office, she informed them that the house had been 'clear of furniture'. While she certainly had an alibi for the period when some of the body parts were thrown into the Clyde, there is the distinct possibility that she could she have assisted in the murder and/or the dismemberment of the body. She obviously knew a lot more about the whole affair than what she was prepared to admit to.

James McKay made Scottish legal history. No convicted person had the right to appeal against their conviction until the Criminal Appeal (Scotland) Act 1926 came into being in October 1926. McKay was the first person sentenced to death to appeal under the legislation. Unfortunately for him, on 29th December 1927, he learned that his appeal had failed and his execution was carried out as decreed on 4th January 1928 in Duke Street Prison.

There is little doubt that James McKay loved both his mother and his wife and undoubtedly his loyalties were torn between the two. It must have been a catastrophic argument between him and his mother which resulted in her murder. But was it his idea alone to dismember the body, burn it and then throw it into the Clyde?

James McKay kept all those secrets to the very end.

66

Chapter 10
Clydebank, August 1931

This case is of interest for many reasons, not least the fact that it caused the law of Scotland to be changed. It also features old-fashioned practices and procedures, which ultimately assisted in bringing the case to a conclusion. Yet, some 75 years after the event, exactly what happened at the scene is still not known for sure. In the far-off days of the first half of the 20th century, being employed as a bank teller was considered to be a superior occupation. Tellers wore suits, starched collars, maybe even a bowler hat and had time to meticulously record the serial numbers of almost every bank note they received or issued in the course of their duties. Wednesday the 12th August 1931 was like any other working day in the town of Clydebank. It was bright and sunny and in the air could be heard the noise of heavy industry from John Brown's shipyard and the constant hum of activity from Singer's factory on Kilbowie Road. The Great Depression had not yet arrived, but it wasn't far off.

Not far from the main entrance of Singer's, a branch of the Clydesdale Bank stood at the corner of Second Avenue and Kilbowie Road. It was known locally as the Radnor Park branch. In charge of the premises was 24-year-old teller Robert Wilson Guthrie Donald. He was the sole bank employee who worked at the branch and he had only recently been promoted into the post. He previously worked as a junior teller at a branch in Auchinleck in Ayrshire, and was described by those who knew him as 'quiet and refined'. He was single and resided with an aunt and uncle in the Hyndland area of the West End of Glasgow. It was expected that he would rise through the ranks of the banking profession without too much difficulty.

The usual procedure was that the bank closed for business every day at three pm. He would then 'cash up' and secure the premises before returning to the main branch on Glasgow Road, Clydebank, to deposit the takings. Doing all this would take almost an hour and Donald was always expected around four pm at the main branch. However, on this particular day, Donald failed to arrive as expected at the main branch. Robert Muir, a junior clerk at the main branch, had telephoned Radnor Park just before 3.10pm to enquire about a customer's account. He spoke with Donald on the telephone for a few minutes. Nothing seemed to be amiss. As time moved slowly on, anxiety levels rose in the main branch and Muir was eventually despatched to the Radnor Park branch. Muir fully expected to meet Donald in the street during his journey but when he arrived at the sub-branch at 4.30pm he was met by the sight of one half of the bank's stout wooden outer doors lying open. Muir moved inside the doors and found the inner glass door open too. Moving further into the bank, Muir could see no trace of his colleague. He did notice a canvas bag lying on top of the counter and believed Donald was probably within the manager's room. He moved forward and was surprised to discover that this door was locked.

As Muir turned, trying to figure out what to do next, his eye caught sight of red stains on the marble floor. These led away from the front door to the far end of the teller's counter. Muir slowly followed the trail and almost collapsed with shock when he found the body of his colleague Donald, crumpled in a heap and bleeding furiously from the head. Muir ran back outside the bank and began shouting for help. Martin Durkin, a tram watchman who was on duty in a hut about 10 yards from the bank's main doors, came at the sound of Muir's cries and together, they entered the bank. Durkin began to comfort the young teller but there wasn't much he could do for Donald's terrible injuries, which appeared to be in the area behind his left ear. Every time Donald moved, however slightly, he moaned in pain. Within ten minutes, Donald died without ever speaking one word about his injuries, how he came by them or who had inflicted them.

A police doctor attended at the scene and pronounced Donald to be dead. However, the ambulance crew who also attended in response to the initial call for assistance was dismissed. Their services were not required at this time. The police, who had been summoned by Muir, arrived just as Donald passed away. They immediately sealed off the premises and awaited the arrival of detectives. Almost immediately, huge crowds gathered as word spread throughout the district. Detectives came and went regularly, their every movement observed by those in the crowd. Flash bulbs momentarily lit up all the windows of the bank as the scene was photographed from every conceivable angle. Each flash was met with a combined intake of breath from the crowd outside, in what was now darkness. Eventually, just before midnight, Donald's body was removed from the bank and taken to the mortuary at Dumbarton. It was from there that the first piece of shocking news in this case was released. Mr Donald had been shot in the head, just above the left eye and the bullet had exited his skull behind his left ear.

Once made aware of this information, the police at the bank carried out a minute search of the walls, floors and fixtures but could find no trace of a bullet. Eventually, they concluded that the assailant who had fired the shot had retrieved the bullet himself and taken it away with him. The police then carried out enquiries with neighbours who resided above the bank premises but not one of them had heard anything untoward. It was noted that a tramcar had broken down right outside the bank about 3.10pm that afternoon and this had attracted quite a crowd, yet not one of them had heard a shot being fired. The tram driver, Frank McGuiggan explained that anyone coming out of the bank at that time would have had an excellent opportunity to merge into the crowd and move away without being noticed.

It was quickly established that £1525 had been taken from the bank, made up of both coins and notes: £240.00 in £20 notes, almost £600 in £5 notes and £300 in £1 notes. The serial numbers of the notes had been recorded and were therefore known. However, whoever was responsible for the crime appeared to have been in some hurry as another £400 in 10-shilling notes, was left lying in the canvas bag on the counter. Even at that time, during the early hours after midnight, various lookouts were broadcast by police. However, people had already been coming forward after hearing of the crime by word of mouth. Miss Agnes Gardiner, a 25-year-old bus conductress from Knightswood contacted the police about nine pm that night and gave a statement. She stated that a male aged about 30 years, 5ft 6in tall and with a cut on the right side of his head, had boarded her Glasgow-bound bus about four pm as it was leaving the Duntocher terminus. Later that night, another witness came forward and stated that a similarly described male, with the same head wound, had got on a bus in Kilbowie Road. This man was carrying an attaché case.

The next morning, Thursday, saw a flurry of activity on the part of the police. One of the first things they did was send out a message to all police forces asking them to be on the alert for a dark-coloured car with the registration number CP 1379, which had been seen heading towards Edinburgh with three men inside. It took a couple of days before it was established that this registration mark had been on a vehicle that had been scrapped three years previously in Halifax. A much stronger lead stemmed from a witness who alleged that while he stood in Kilbowie Road opposite the bank, he saw a male push open the bank doors. Two other men then came out, one of whom was holding a handkerchief to his face, which appeared to be bleeding. The men then separated each going into different tenement closes on Kilbowie Road. These closes lead through to a patch of derelict land at the rear of the building, where the men could have met up again, out of view of anyone.

The above details appeared to tie in with information given to police that three deserters from the Cameronian regiment, currently stationed at the Wyndford Barracks Maryhill in Glasgow, had been seen in Clydebank the night before the murder. As a result, the police wished to interview the three men, and named them as Enoch Stevenson, aged 21 and 5ft 10in in height with blue eyes, from Bullwell in Nottinghamshire; John Brown, 20 years old with brown eyes and a native of Coatbridge and lastly Thomas Henderson, 18 years of age with green eyes, originally from Gateshead.

Other snippets of information were coming to light also. A man had attended the greyhound race meeting at Clydeholm Stadium in Clydebank on Wednesday night. He was given a Clydesdale Bank £1 note in his winnings and thought that it was bloodstained. He handed the bank note to police the following morning. Again, on Wednesday, a woman walked into a chemist's shop in Partick and bought a two-ounce packet of cotton wool. The purchase price was sixpence, yet the woman proffered a Clydesdale Bank £5 note in payment; the note was retained by police due to it having 'one or two dark marks, which resembled bloodstains'. Police started to try and trace the woman. Perhaps the fact that the Clydesdale Bank had offered a reward of £200 for information had something to do with the number of witnesses who had come forward.

Thursday morning saw the postmortem on Donald's corpse performed by pathologists Professor John Glaister and Dr John Anderson, and although the results were not made public for a number of days, word soon became public that Donald had been shot twice; once above the left eye, as first thought, and once behind the left ear. This latter wound had earlier been considered as an exit wound. Two bullets were recovered from Donald's body; one from his skull and the other from his throat, where it had lodged. Some rumours suggested that the murder was the work of a gang of men while others seemed to favour that only one man was responsible. Even police spokesmen could not agree on a common opinion. No matter, the Clydesdale Bank quickly increased their reward to £500.

The Clydebank police did all the usual things that police do after a serious crime has been committed. They 'combed out' all the criminals from the lodging houses and dwelling houses in the rougher parts of the locality. Some of them were taken to the local office for interview, but none appeared to even merit the title of suspect. One of those detained later gave the local newspaper an interview on his release. Describing himself as 'a former crook with more than 45 years experience of crime and criminals', he declared that the crime had been committed by amateurs because it had been quickly planned and crudely carried out. Furthermore, he was certain that it had been the work of three men, two who actually carried out the crime and one who acted as a guard to prevent interference from outside. Perhaps he had previously read the newspaper reports of the Kilbowie Road witness?

All of this police activity was to no avail; very quickly, leads dried up. Suspects had alibis, which turned out to be unshakeable. Even when the police traced and interviewed the three deserters from Wyndford Barracks, they had alibis which stood up to scrutiny. They were returned after police interview to suffer army punishment. No stolen money was turning up in the hands of shopkeepers or publicans. Just as public interest in matter seemed to be waning, police received an unexpected public offer of help. Mrs Annie Mason of Ibrox, Glasgow, or as she was better known, Madam Victoria, was a self-proclaimed clairvoyant. She quite openly stated that her 'feelings' were that the crime had been committed by a 'gang of hardened desperados'. However, she was quick to cover that statement by adding that a 'gang' could quite easily consist of 'one person only'! She also stated that on the day of the crime, she had experienced a 'dull ache in her head' and that she knew 'something bad was happening somewhere.' Her offer of help was politely declined. And so, ever so slowly, the murder of the 24-year-old bank teller Robert Donald faded from public memory.

By December 1931 all work on the Cunarder *Queen Mary* at John Brown's shipyard in Clydebank was suspended and thousands of workers were laid off. The Great Depression was starting to bite. It wouldn't be until it was well and truly over that the next instalment in this case would become known. Just a couple of days before the end of 1936, a Bank of England £5 note was returned to bank headquarters in London to be withdrawn and destroyed. As was usual, the serial number was checked and this revealed that it was one of the notes stolen from the Radnor Park branch in August 1931. In those days, a Bank of England note never went back into circulation after being returned to bank headquarters. The old note would be withdrawn and incinerated and a new note would be issued in its place. When a Bank of England note was handed into any other bank, the person depositing it was expected to sign the rear of the note, which was then sent to London. Once there, the serial numbers were compared to lists held by the bank. This particular £5 note was traced to Lewis's Polytechnic warehouse in Glasgow where it had been used for a pre-Christmas purchase. Within days, another Bank of England £5 note from the robbery turned up, having been used in a

Clydebank Co-operative store. Extensive enquiries were made at both stores and eventually led police to an address in Glasgow, very near to the boundary with Clydebank.

Early on the morning of 6th January 1937, uniformed police and detectives converged on a top-floor flat at 2327 Dumbarton Road, Yoker, Glasgow. After gaining entry, the officers found only a 40-year-old female – Ethel Burke – present. The house was searched and between £300 and £400 was found. Burke was arrested and taken to Clydebank Police Station. Whatever happened at the police office is open to interpretation, but the police later returned to the house that day and discovered another quantity of bank notes and a pistol. In total, £610 was recovered, including two bundles of 20 £5 Clydesdale Bank notes and one bundle of 20 £5 Bank of England notes. The pistol was a .32 calibre, five-shot revolver of American make. It was quite an old weapon and had seen much use but was in very good working condition. When found, it was loaded and wrapped in an oil cloth for protection. Later that day, Ethel Burke was charged with three counts of resetting stolen bank notes and appeared in court at Dumbarton. She was remanded in custody for further enquiry and sent to Duke Street Prison.

Within days, police were satisfied that they had solved the five-year-old mystery and they sent a report to the procurator fiscal, who in turn forwarded it to the Crown Office. The report contained the name of a male as the person responsible for shooting and murdering Robert Donald and robbing him of £1525. The police were satisfied that they had recovered the murder weapon and most of the stolen money and that only one man had committed the crime. The Crown Office made no official statement on the matter and maintained that stance throughout. Even when questions were asked in the House of Commons about the case, the official line still was one of 'no comment'. This stems from the Crown's practice of never making a statement or announcement on any matter not yet before a court of law. Seventy-eight years after the crime it can now be revealed not only why the arrest of the murderer was never pursued, but also his identity.

The name of the murderer of Robert Donald was William Burke, elder brother of Ethel Burke.

Burke's family came to live at 2327 Dumbarton Road Glasgow in 1916. The family consisted of Mrs Burke and her two sons, Alfred and William and daughter Ethel. Just after the end of the Great War, the two sons went to America to make their fortunes. William never did and became homesick, returning home for a short time in 1921. However, he couldn't find any work and returned to America, only to return home permanently in 1929 when he

72

learned that his mother was seriously ill. His mother did succumb to her illness that year and almost immediately after this, Ethel also became ill to such an extent that she could never work again. William took up residence with his sister and made attempts at getting work while looking after her. He gained employment with several local engineering firms but it was only on a part-time basis. With neither he nor his sister working, money would have been tight for them.

And so, on the afternoon of Wednesday 12th August 1931, William Burke found himself in the vicinity of the Clydesdale Bank on Kilbowie Road in nearby Clydebank. He had his American-made .32 revolver in his pocket. The bank closed at three pm. and he waited patiently outside, probably watching the commotion surrounding the broken down tramcar. As Donald opened the main doors of the bank on his way out, he was confronted by Burke who was pointing the pistol directly at him. Donald was forced back inside the bank and a struggle ensued between the two men.

While Donald had earlier been described as 'quiet and refined', he has also been described in one report as a 'fairly hefty youth', who, in his spare time, played rugby at a decent level. Without doubt, he was the younger and stronger man. However, at some point, Burke got the upper hand, striking Donald several times in the face, probably with the pistol, and then shooting him in the forehead, just above the left eye. Donald slumped down onto the floor behind the inner doors.

Burke quickly picked up Donald's briefcase, which contained the cash that was being transferred to the main branch, placed it on the teller's counter and started looking through its contents. Donald however, was not dead. He began crawling across the marble floor towards the far end of the counter, where the telephone was located. Burke noticed this and quite callously stood over Donald and shot him for a second time, this time behind the left ear.

Burke then picked up the briefcase and its contents and hurriedly exited the bank. In his haste, he left one of the main front doors lying open. Where Burke went after this point is open to conjecture. We know for definite that Donald was intercepted on his way out of the premises for two reasons. First, Muir spoke with Donald at 3.10pm which is a full ten minutes after closing time. Second, the blinds on the bank's windows had been pulled down. This was a ritual that other bank staff were able to confirm and which Donald carried out every day. It was the last thing he did, moments before locking up the bank.

We also know that Donald had pulled himself across the floor rather than having been dragged. The trail of blood was concentrated in some places, suggesting that Donald paused at times in his efforts. If his body had been dragged by his attacker, the blood trail would have been uniformly dispersed. It would also cover the attacker in blood. Dragging a body with a head wound by the feet would result in an unsmeared blood trail.

Burke made good his escape without being noticed. There is every likelihood that he was the man with the head wound who was seen on two different buses within a short period of time. The first bus took him north in Kilbowie Road, and away from the local police office which was situated in Hall Street which was south of the bank. Like today's bus services, the one in 1931 was a local service which went no further than nearby Duntocher, where Burke changed buses and travelled on the Glasgow-bound bus, whose route incidentally, did not go anywhere near Kilbowie Road. Within an hour of committing the crime, Burke was still undetected and probably climbing the stairs to his home. Burke would not have left his house for the next month or so, until both the furore over the outrage had abated and his head wound had healed.

In April 1935, William Burke collapsed in the street near his home and was taken to the Western Infirmary in Glasgow, where doctors diagnosed 'shock'. We know it better today as a 'heart attack'. Without regaining consciousness, Burke died later that evening from heart failure with his sister as his bedside. After his death, nothing much changed in the life of Ethel Burke, although neighbours later stated that she became more reclusive. It wasn't until the lead up to Christmas 1936 that Ethel decided to spend some of the large denomination notes taken in the robbery and this led to her eventual detection. Perhaps it was only at this time that she discovered the money in her house?

Although she was charged with a number of serious offences, Ethel was found insane and unfit to stand trial. She was committed to an asylum for the rest of her life. Questions on the case were raised in the House of Commons in response to newspaper speculation. However, ministers were only allowed to reiterate the Crown Office's practice of not commenting on matters not yet before a court of law. The matter rested there, as the authorities could not bring a dead man to trial.

The case also brought about a change in the law. Within two years of the murder it became illegal for banks to open for business without at least two members of staff being present on the premises, although some banks previously operated this policy on a voluntary basis.

Chapter 11
Cowcaddens, January 1932

Elizabeth Campbell was 24 years of age and stayed with her elderly aunt and uncle at 11 Wemyss Street in Cowcaddens, Glasgow. She had lodged there for nearly eight years, ever since she was orphaned by the death of her mother in 1924. Elizabeth, or 'Lizzie' as she was known, was deaf in one ear and totally blind in her right eye. Even so, she worked full time in Buchanan's sweet factory in Stewart Street, Cowcaddens and had a small circle of friends. By all accounts Lizzie was an obliging type of person. Her elderly aunt was very ill, and had been for some time, which meant that she couldn't attend to her employment as a cleaner at the typewriter supply company of Farquharson Brothers at 191 Hope Street in Glasgow city centre. Lizzie took on her aunt's work commitments and would attend and clean their offices after finishing her own shift at the sweet factory. It was said that Lizzie enjoyed the work and took pride in it.

So why was this shy, timid and helpful young woman was found gagged, bound and battered to death on Sunday 31st January 1932 in the offices she cleaned, all for a robbery that netted those responsible the grand sum of 3s 9d in cash, or 19p in today's money. She had suffered almost 20 blows to her head and face, her spectacles were broken and torn from her face and her false teeth had been knocked from her mouth. But who could have done such a thing? Was there one killer or a gang of them? The police were baffled and began trying to unravel Lizzie's movements prior to her death.

Lizzie finished her Saturday morning shift at the sweet factory and after a bit of lunch at home, she left to go to her scheduled afternoon cleaning at Farquharson's. She told her aunt that she would be home just before six pm, as she had made arrangements to go to the pictures with her friend, Betty Martin and would be meeting her at the house in Wemyss Street. Six pm came, and so to did Betty Martin, but Lizzie never turned up. Her uncle, Thomas Campbell, told Betty that he had met up with an acquaintance of his at Central Station at about four pm that afternoon and had passed the Farquharson offices. He had knocked on the window and was greeted with a cheery wave of recognition from Lizzie. He passed the offices later, about five pm, and saw that they were in darkness and assumed that Lizzie had finished for the day and gone home.

By eight pm, those who were waiting were worried. Her uncle Thomas, along with Betty, went to Farquharson's offices and looked through the windows and into the darkness of the premises. From what they could see, everything was in order but Lizzie was nowhere to be seen. The doors to the offices were also secure. Both then left the scene, totally confused as to where Lizzie might be. The best idea they could think of was that Lizzie had gone to visit some relatives but had forgotten to tell anyone. There appeared to be nothing that the relatives or friends could do except wait until Lizzie either returned home or got in touch somehow.

By the following morning, Lizzie had done neither, so her uncle once again called at the offices in Hope Street and again he peered in the windows. He saw nothing untoward. He had no option but to call at the Central Police Station and report his niece as a missing person. After this, he went to a house in Garscube Road, in the Maryhill area and informed Lizzie's brother, William, of what had happened. Together, the two men returned to the offices and met up with a uniformed policeman, who was standing outside. All three then began looking in all of the windows of the building and thanks to the daylight, were able to see further into the dark, gloomy interior. Almost immediately, it was seen that a drawer of one of the desks was fully opened. Closer observation revealed Lizzie's spectacles lying on the floor near the desk. Clearly, something was amiss, although they assumed that Lizzie had merely taken ill and perhaps fallen over.

Keys to the offices were sent for, and when they arrived, the police officer was the first to enter. What he found inside was enough for him to usher Thomas and William Campbell back out of the premises and order them to go to the police office to get further assistance. The officer had found Lizzie lying on her back, her mouth gagged and her hands tied behind her back. She had been severely beaten about the head and face and she was dead. The office was in a state of disarray. Desk drawers were open and papers scattered on the floor; the safe was lying open. Soon, detectives were swarming all over the scene. Professor Glaister Jnr visited the offices and examined Lizzie's corpse. He told police that in his opinion, death had occurred the previous evening, probably around six or seven pm and the cause of death was that she had been beaten to death.

The police had very little to go on. The entire office area was finger-printed, but that resulted in hundreds of impressions being obtained. This was a time-consuming exercise as each impression had to be compared to each other and then with the police fingerprint files. On the plus side, they had quickly recovered what was believed to be the murder weapon, a black ebonite ruler, which was found covered in blood, lying not far from Lizzie's body. Also, it quickly became evident that the motive for the murder of Lizzie Campbell was robbery. Two cash boxes were missing from the safe, the keys to which had been kept in a drawer in one of the desks; it was estimated that the money in the cash boxes could be considered small change. The murder investigation was splashed across the front pages of Scotland's newspapers, all of them asking the same question ... whodunnit?

On Monday morning, and for most of the day, police interviewed all staff members who worked in the offices but no suspects were revealed. A number of potential witnesses from outwith Farquharson's workforce came forward to tell police their stories. One woman stated that she had been walking in Hope Street about 5.30pm on the Saturday evening when she saw two males coming out of the offices. They stopped momentarily to lock the doors and then walked off down Hope Street to the south. One of the males was carrying a box about the size of a biscuit tin. She provided police with physical descriptions of the men, and these were published in the later Monday editions of the newspapers. An appeal for information was also made at the same time. The police then interviewed two men who had been working all day on Saturday in the building next door to Farquharson's, but they had heard absolutely nothing untoward during the day, possibly because of the traffic noise from busy Hope Street.

The two stolen cash boxes were found on Monday morning by park worker Robert Wylie; they were lying hidden in bushes in Kelvingrove Park, open and empty. Wylie's attention had been attracted by a broken wooden handle from some kind of tool that was left nearby on some grass. The handle was covered in blood. Although they had witnesses and descriptions of possible suspects, the police investigations were not going forward with any momentum. However, on Tuesday 2nd February, a breakthrough occurred.

In the sack load of mail delivered to the Central Police Station was a letter, unsigned and postmarked 'Glasgow, February 1st 10pm'. The letter contained a short statement, which read: 'If you question the boy McCudden in St Peter's Street, who works in Farquharson' brothers, you might find out something in connection with the Hope Street murder.' Det Supt Forbes, who was in charge of the investigation, sent out officers to St Peter's Street and George McCudden, an 18-year-old office boy with Farquharson's, was brought back to the police office. McCudden was told that the police wanted to go over the statement he had given earlier. Once at the police office, McCudden was duly interrogated.

He eventually admitted his involvement and as a consequence of his confession, police officers visited two more addresses in the St George's Cross area of the city and detained another two youths. Andrew Allison Cameron and John Kirton, both 18 years old and both of Balnain Street, were arrested and after questioning, all three were charged with murdering Elizabeth Campbell by beating her to death. They also faced three charges of theft in relation to the cash boxes. All three appeared in court the following day and were remanded in custody, pending further inquiry.

Inquiries were then made into statements made by McCudden and Cameron regarding Kirton which suggested that Kirton had played no part in the murder as he had only been a lookout, stationed outside the offices in Hope Street; he had never entered the office at any time and had been unaware of any violence used. As a result, Kirton was released from prison, all charges against him having been dropped. He then became the prosecution's chief witness and was one of the first to give evidence when the trial of McCudden and Cameron began in the North Court of Glasgow High Court on Monday 18th April 1932. Lord Blackburn presided over the event.

A strange episode took place at the start of the trial. The defence teams, between them, objected to the eight women who had been selected to serve on the jury. Eight challenges were the limit, and after this, another female was selected to serve. As she would be the only female on the jury, the judge said that he would be prepared to excuse her jury service, if she so desired. The woman stated that she would prefer to be discharged and her place was taken by a male juror so the jury was now made up of 15 men.

What became obvious very early in the trial was that the police had made extensive inquiries since the arrest of McCudden and Cameron. A procession of witnesses gave evidence. Nineteen-year-old newsvendor Edward Gorrell stated that he knew both accused youths. He saw both youths in Hope Street on the afternoon of the murder, and again later that day when he was on a tram passing Farquharson's, he saw both standing in the doorway of the offices. Miss Christina Cooper told the court that she had been passing the office on the Saturday afternoon in question and saw the two youths standing in the doorway of Farquharson's and that they were 'carrying on and joking'.

John Kirton was, of course, the star witness for the Crown. His evidence began with a conversation he had with McCudden in a billiards hall in St Peter's Street. McCudden had asked him to 'watch cops' for him while he

(McCudden) and Cameron broke into an office. McCudden said that it was his own office and that there would be a woman cleaner in the office at the time but that she was deaf and blind and wouldn't bother them. They were to slip into one of the rooms and wait until the woman finished her work and left. In the event, Kirton became frightened and ran off during the break-in and met up later that Saturday night with Cameron, who showed him his bloodstained jacket sleeve. Cameron said it had come from the woman as he held her head. Later that same night, Kirton met up with McCudden, who told him that the woman had 'flown at him' and he had to fight her off. The woman had bitten him on the hand and it had swollen up quite badly. McCudden continued that he had then tied her up, put his handkerchief in her mouth to quieten her and then beaten her with a hard rubber ruler.

John Birnie, a spirit salesman from Buccleugh Street, told the court that he was a regular patron of the billiards hall in St Peter's Street. He knew both McCudden and Cameron and had spoken to them regularly. He revealed to a hushed courtroom that he was present in the billiards hall when McCudden came in about 6.30pm on the Saturday in question. McCudden seemed to him to be in an agitated or excited state and when he asked him why, McCudden answered that he had been in a fight in his office. He went on adding that the woman in the office had been screaming 'Murder! Murder!' so he hit her and 'gave her a good hiding.' He then gagged her and tied her up. McCudden also said at one point that she was a 'gone coon.'

After they fled the scene, he and Andy Cameron went to Kelvingrove Park where they opened one of the cash boxes with a key and hid the other one in some shrubbery because the key wouldn't open that one. The opened cash box contained three shillings and nine pence in loose change.

Birnie saw both McCudden and Cameron in the billiards hall next on the Monday night. By this time, the murder was all over the newspapers and common knowledge. Cameron appeared withdrawn and spoke to no one while McCudden gabbed with a number of people, the topic being the murder. Birnie claimed he could not help but listen to the conversation and was horrified to hear him give out details of the murder. At one stage, he told McCudden to, 'shut up and go home,' as he thought that if McCudden continued talking like that, then he would 'make a mess of it and give himself away.'

Another witness, Matthew McCann, a near neighbour of Andrew Cameron, stated that he had been told by both accused that the two of them had jumped on the woman in the office and while McCudden punched and kicked her, Cameron bound and gagged her. McCann also went with them to recover the second cash box from the park grounds. This was on the Sunday night. The key broke in the lock and McCudden had to break it open using a file, from which the handle broke off. The cash box only contained sheets of postage stamps and receipts. McCudden split the contents between McCann and Cameron and that was the reason for McCann's arrest. However, when he handed over his share of the stamps and gave the police a statement, he was released from custody.

Next up was the medical evidence. The death of Lizzie Campbell was caused due to shock and heart failure brought on by severe injuries to the head and face and to blood loss. Eleven separate blows to the face were recorded by doctors during the postmortem examination. At some places on the woman's face, clear indentations of shoe or boot marks were visible, suggesting that she had been kicked hard. A further seven wounds or injuries were noted to the head and skull area. These could not have been caused by the deceased falling over.

The remainder of the medical evidence concerned the mental state of both accused. Professor John Glaister Snr had been instructed by the procurator fiscal's department to visit with and examine both accused youths while they were held in custody in Barlinnie Prison. He found that both were perfectly normal and competent and exhibited absolutely no evidence of any mental abnormality. (This was one of the last occasions that Professor Glaister gave evidence at the High Court as he passed away in December 1932, aged 76 years.)

Only three witnesses were called to assist the defence case. McCudden's sister, the scoutmaster of the scout troop of which McCudden had been a member and Dr Gilbert Garry, chief medical officer at Duke Street Prison. The first two spoke of the previous good character of McCudden, while the latter witness stated that McCudden had a rather detached manner and did not seem to appreciate the gravity of the situation he was now in. Dr Garry added that McCudden appeared to be strangely pleased with himself. In the case of Cameron, the opinion was that his outlook in life was a childish one. The trial concluded with counsel and the judge's summing up. The jury were asked to retire to consider their verdicts and they took only 50 minutes to return to court with a majority verdict of guilty on both accused on the murder charge. However, the jury were unanimous in recommending mercy for both accused. On the remaining three charges of theft, the jury were unanimous in their guilty verdicts.

The advocate depute called for the judge to pass sentence but only on the murder charge. Both accused stood stock-still in the dock, the only evidence of tension being McCudden gripping and ungripping the brass railing atop the dock. Cameron appeared to onlookers to have a flushed face and moved his lips slightly, as if they were dry. Lord Blackburn took the opportunity to make his displeasure known. He noted the jury's recommendation for mercy but he stated that McCudden and Cameron should not put too much faith in that clause because they had been found guilty of a deliberate, cowardly and callous murder and it might be deemed that they were not deserving of any clemency.

Elizabeth Campbell was murdered because she chose to fight back against her attackers. She was brutally done to death by two youths, who it appeared to some, showed a cruel indifference to all consequences. Nonetheless, the recommendation for mercy would be forwarded to the appropriate authority. Lord Blackburn then pronounced sentence of death on both McCudden and Cameron and set the date for execution as 11th May at Barlinnie Prison.

Immediately, a petition was raised in relation to quashing the sentence of death. In a little over two weeks, an amazing 60,000 people had signed the petition before it was forwarded to the Secretary of State for Scotland. On 8th May 1932, the baby-faced killers of Elizabeth 'Lizzie' Campbell were reprieved. Their death sentences were replaced with ones of penal servitude for life.

Chapter 12
Scotstoun, March 1935

At nine pm on the 4th March 1935 in Scotstoun, in the West End of Glasgow, it was cold, dark and drizzling. As the usual flow of people went about their business the only sound was the clatter of the coming and going of tramcars along Dumbarton Road. It all appeared to be a normal Monday night until the loud noise of a gunshot echoed from wet pavement to tenement wall and then into every close in the district. Those walking in the street stopped and turned to where they believed the sound had come from. Most didn't even realise that the noise they had heard was a gunshot. As everyone stared at each other, looking for confirmation of what they had heard, two men ran from the doorway of the grocer's shop at 1517 Dumbarton Road and into nearby Earl Place. One of the men appeared to be trying to conceal a large pistol within his raincoat as he fled.

One witness, 15-year-old William Cameron, who had been walking along Dumbarton Road, near to the shop, gave chase to the two men, although he later admitted that he didn't know exactly why he was chasing after them. By the time he reached the corner of Earl Place, about 30 yards away, he had lost sight of them both. Similarly, a police officer, who had been a passenger on a passing tramcar, gave chase but he too discovered that, on running into Earl Place, the men were nowhere to be seen. While Cameron stopped, the policeman continued into Earl Street, where the tenement houses had only recently been constructed, but there was still no sign of them. The policeman returned to Dumbarton Road and found that a large crowd had already gathered outside the grocer's shop. As he pushed his way through, he found a couple of bystanders tending to David Bayne, the elderly owner of the business. He was lying in the doorway of the shop, on his back, and unmistakably dead. A large bloodstain covered his chest and blood had pooled on the ground at the entrance to the shop.

Very quickly, detectives from the Marine Division, Partick, were on the scene and began taking statements from all those who had witnessed even the most trivial of events. As this was going on, other detectives from the Flying Squad began a door-to-door search for the two men thought to be responsible for Bayne's murder. Houses in the surrounding area, but especially in Earl Place and Earl Street, were searched from top to bottom. Police patrols in unmarked squad cars were stepped up, as all available police personnel were rushed to the area. They kept watch on railway and bus stations, the docks and searched lodging houses all over the city. Numerous residents of these dwellings were questioned, some at great length, but nothing came of this.

However, within a few hours, police had discovered a number of facts, which had come from their interviews with witnesses. They determined that David Bayne closed his shop every night at seven pm when he sent his two young female assistants home. However, he then had a peculiar habit of staying behind in the shop, counting the day's takings and reviewing orders. He remained in full view of anyone passing on the street outside, because he would never pull down the shop window blinds. Occasionally, a passing customer would stop and tap on the window, to be greeted by a wave of recognition from the genial businessman. One witness, who had been waiting for a tram, reported seeing two men loitering in the doorway of Bayne's shop, but thought only that they were sheltering from the rain. She looked away, heard the gunshot and when she looked back, saw the men running away from the shop. The witness ran to the open doorway of the shop just in time to see Mr Bayne stagger out of the shop onto the pavement. He managed to blurt out 'Police!' before collapsing into the arms of the witness.

Mr Bayne's body lay in the shop doorway for most of the night until it was examined by Dr John Anderson, pathologist and Mr Muir, acting procurator fiscal. Dr Anderson found that Bayne had been shot once through the heart and had bled to death. After the cursory examination, Muir gave instructions for the body to be removed to a place inside the shop, out of the rain. At the postmortem examination, it was found that the bullet had ricocheted around inside Bayne's body and finally came to rest at the top of his right leg, from where it was removed. When it was examined closely, it was found to be of .45 calibre.

Although police later publicly announced that robbery was the obvious motive for the shooting, in actual fact, nothing had been stolen from the grocer. The police found all of the money that Bayne had been counting moments before his murder, lying on the shop counter, neatly stacked and untouched. Also, Bayne's wallet was still within his jacket pocket. Although 60 years of age, David Bayne was a gentle giant of a man, standing over 6ft 4in tall and built proportionately. He was well known to all in the community and especially by those who frequented his shop, as a quiet and even-tempered man. He was a widower who had a married daughter but he didn't see much of her, mainly because she lived outside Glasgow and Bayne was a workaholic who opened his shop seven days a week. Officers worked late into the night at the scene of the crime. The shop counter, doorway and most especially, the front window of the store, were dusted for fingerprints. A substantial number of impressions were obtained from this exercise.

The day after the murder, Tuesday, was spent by police following up leads, mainly produced in response to the published descriptions of the two men wanted in connection with the murder. All of the witnesses interviewed were able to provide descriptions of the two men, and from them the following was circulated.

Both wanted men were aged between 20 and 25 years of age. One was about 5ft 6in in height, the other being about 5ft 4in or 5in. The taller of the two was of medium build with dark features and was said to be 'well-spoken'. The second man was of slim build with reddish coloured hair and a fresh complexion. Both were wearing raincoats and soft caps. As one of the wanted men was described as 'well-spoken', a witness must have heard at least one of them speaking. A review of the available witness statements taken by police reveals that no such thing was reported. Nonetheless, this part of the description endured and was repeated on every occasion that the descriptions were reiterated.

As a result of these being released, a strange story reached the ears of the detectives. A man had come forward to relate to police that about eight pm on Monday night, about an hour before the shooting, he had disturbed two men breaking into his home in Danes Drive, which is less than half a mile from the grocer's shop. He hadn't bothered to report the matter at the time, but now that he had heard the descriptions of the men involved in the murder, he realised that it fitted those of the two would-be housebreakers. Police fingerprint experts swarmed all over the man's house, attempting to find any impressions that would match some of those taken from the grocer's shop.

Later on Tuesday evening, a postcard was delivered to Partick Police Station in Anderson Street. Its contents gave the detectives hope of an early conclusion to the case. The postcard named two local men as being those responsible for the murder and then continued on to provide police with details that only they knew about. This information was, quite simply, that the murder weapon was a .45 revolver. Police activity in the Scotstoun area was stepped up even further as a result of the postcard's contents, and within a few hours, the men named in the postcard had been located and detained. They were taken to Partick Police Station and questioned at length during the night. Their stories were checked and re-checked and eventually confirmed. Disheartened detectives released both men in the early hours of Wednesday morning.

After the initial surge of activity and information, the police were struggling to maintain momentum in the inquiry. While the main contents of the postcard proved false, they still appealed for the writer of the postcard to make further contact with them, as they were anxious to know how the writer knew about the calibre of the weapon. They also appealed for anyone who may have seen anything suspicious in the vicinity of both the River Clyde and the local canals, or any other places where disposal of a firearm might be possible. As with any case that receives widespread publicity, and especially one where the police have appealed for information, the detectives were soon inundated with scores of anonymous letters, all proffering advice and 'information'. Precious time was wasted with officers delegated to read these letters before they were summarily dismissed as useless to the investigation.

Late on Wednesday night, a new witness came forward and provided a startling statement. She stated that about five minutes before the murder, she passed the shop and saw two men standing in the doorway. As she passed, she thought she recognised one of the men and nodded to him. However, when she received no acknowledgement in return, she looked at the men closer and realised that she had been mistaken. However, having had such a close look at the men, she was able to assure police that she would be able to identify the men again. The police believed that this witness's story enhanced their opinion that the men responsible for the crime lived locally. It reconciled with the fact that the men were able to disappear so easily after the crime and the belief, in some police quarters, that the men were being shielded by family or friends in the Scotstoun area. Somewhat unusually, but probably as a consequence of the importance of her statement and that fact that she too lived locally, the police refused to give out any personal details of their 'star' witness.

This new information gave a different bearing and a fresh impetus to the murder inquiry and about two am on Friday 8th March 1935, an arrest was made. Police, in large numbers, swooped on a house in Earl Street and rudely awakened the occupants. One, 25-year-old Thomas McAleer, was detained and removed to the local police office, where within the hour, he was charged with the murder of David Bayne. As a direct result of McAleer's arrest, several of his friends were also detained and put on identity parades but none were picked out. Later that morning, McAleer appeared in the Marine Divisional Police Court, where he was again formally charged. McAleer was not asked to answer the charge and stood in the dock throughout the short hearing with his arms folded tightly across his chest, staring straight at the magistrate on the bench. He was remanded in custody for further inquiry and ushered back to the cells.

Later that afternoon, the funeral cortege of Mr Bayne travelled from his home in Polnoon Avenue in Knightswood to the Western Necropolis. The service was a very private affair with only a few personal friends in attendance. Although the weather was again inclement, quite a large crowd of spectators had gathered in the roadway outside the house and many had brought wreaths to the scene. The majority of the crowd were women and most could be identified as customers of the shop. As soon as the cortege moved off, the crowd dispersed quietly and quickly. At the same time as the funeral was taking place, police were hard at work with inquiries centred on McAleer's movements on the night of the murder. He was claiming that he had an alibi and when the police checked his claims, they found that they were true. McAleer had numerous witnesses who confirmed that he was nowhere near the murder scene the previous Monday night. He was, in fact, present at a whist drive elsewhere in Scotstoun.

As a result of these inquiries, the lack of evidence meant that McAleer was released from custody on Saturday morning. Again, a large crowd had gathered in the vicinity of the police office, expecting or hoping for further developments in the case. McAleer was allowed to exit the police station via a side door and was able to avoid the crowd.

Due to a combination of the scant public interest shown in the case, the lack of any tangible, solid evidence or information coming to light and to keep the case at the forefront of the news and public's mind, Glasgow Corporation took the unprecedented step of offering a £500 reward for information leading to the conviction of those responsible. As expected, when the news of the offer of a reward for information was made public, all sorts of it, good and bad, came the way of the detectives. A quantity of bullets was discovered in the Forth and Clyde Canal at Firhill Bridge and a full-scale search of the canal and its many basins near this location was carried out. The banks of the waterway were also searched, all in an effort to locate the gun. While this looked like a possible breakthrough in the case, the reality was that while the bullets found were of .45 calibre, they were of a different brand to the one used to kill Bayne.

All registered gun owners in the north and west of Glasgow were visited by police in the hope of discovering if any weapons had been stolen but not reported. What happened during these inquiries was that the police were then handed a substantial number of revolvers which had been kept as souvenirs from the Great War, thus adding to the growing mountain of useless information they were dealing with.

The fingerprint search had produced no suspects either. All prints recovered had been checked against those held on file at police headquarters, but with a negative result. Even the comparisons between the impressions from the grocer's shop and the house in Danes Drive showed no similarities. With these failures, police openly admitted that the men were not known to them. As with all cases of murder, if there are no arrests within a reasonable period of time, then incoming information will slowly grind to a halt. And so it was with the murder of David Bayne. All too soon, leads dried up and detectives were taken off the case and assigned to other ongoing or new cases.

Bayne's attackers were never caught. At this date, there is no chance, based on the available evidence, of anyone ever being identified as being responsible.

The case remains unsolved.

Chapter 13

- -

Partick, August 1937

What are the demons that possess some people and move them to acts of madness, creating misery and suffering for so many others? In Glasgow, there is no better example of this than the sad tale of Upendra Ranjan Biswas, a 30-year-old native of Calcutta who graduated from that city's university in 1933 and came to Scotland to teach. He enrolled in teacher training courses at Jordanhill College and secured himself a job at Barrhead High School. Biswas was quickly accepted and settled into life in Glasgow.

Biswas was a keen athlete and maintained an interest in most sports while teaching. Late in 1935, he travelled to Sweden to take part in some seasonal winter sports. Life would appear to have been extremely hectic for Biswas at this time, for on 18th July 1936, he married his 17-year-old sweetheart, Alma Millar, at Partick Old Parish Church. Alma's family resided locally and her parents were well respected in the community. Her father was a dentist and operated his practice from their home at 1 Lawrence Street, Partick. But the newly married couple did not take up residence within the Millar household, instead staying in a number of rented accommodations across the city. By all accounts, this was a result of tension in the Millar family over their daughter's choice of husband. Two weeks after the wedding, when Biswas and some friends attended the Olympic Games, as spectators, in Berlin, Alma stayed behind. She was 17 and four months pregnant at the time of the wedding.

This situation horrified her parents and left them open to ridicule and shame. While Alma's condition possibly was not evident at the wedding, there were understandable misgivings due to the shortness of the engagement and the age gap between bride and groom. In December 1936, Alma gave birth to a healthy baby boy, who they named Amal Biswas. Within a few months of the birth, cracks began appearing in the marriage and after one argument too many, Alma and her child left her husband and took up residence with her family at Lawrence Street in the West End of Glasgow.

Not much appears to have happened in the first few months of the separation. Biswas continued with his teaching post and moved into lodgings at 5 Belmont Street, Glasgow, most likely to be nearer to his wife and child, who he saw regularly. Biswas was besotted with his wife and child. About three weeks before the tragedy struck, Alma was sent on a short break by her family. She took her son and spent some time living in a hotel in Arrochar. Biswas was told about the holiday but not the exact location.

He and a friend then hired a Glasgow taxicab, blacked out its windows using crepe paper and toured hotels in the Helensburgh, Rhu and Garelochhead areas, looking to locate his wife. He didn't find her and had to return to Glasgow defeated and visibly unhappy about the entire affair.

What seems to have been the catalyst for the events of Wednesday evening, 11th August 1937, began the day before at Glasgow Sheriff Court when Alma Biswas started formal divorce proceedings. Sheriff Robertson heard the case and ordered that defences be lodged and continued the case for further inquiry. For Biswas, this was the final straw. Whether or not he had a premeditated plan is unknown, but he hailed a taxicab in Hope Street, near Central Station and instructed the driver, Thomas Strawbridge, to take him to Lawrence Street at the corner with Byres Road. Strawbridge was a veteran taxi driver of almost 25 years and something made him suspicious of his passenger. Perhaps it was the way Biswas had barked his instructions at him or perhaps it was the way he was taking large gulps from a bottle of wine as he sat in the back of the taxi.

It was a fine, sunny summer evening and just after six pm Alma Biswas was sitting in a chair at the open window of the sitting room of the first-floor apartment. She was aware that her estranged husband was coming to visit her and she was looking out for him. Her viewpoint allowed her to see in almost every direction and therefore cover every approach to the house. Very soon, Biswas arrived in the taxi and as he paid Strawbridge, Alma ran down the stairs in an attempt to either keep him from the house or to speak to him prior to his visit. Biswas ran across the road just as Alma exited from the close mouth. Without even a word passing between them, Biswas pulled out a pistol from under his jacket, took aim and shot his wife. She slumped slowly to the ground, trying to grasp some railings to break her fall.

Strawbridge, who had been watching from his cab, immediately sprang into action, leapt from his cab and rushed across the roadway. Biswas was aware that Strawbridge was making a dive for him and fired his gun, hitting the driver square in the chest. Strawbridge halted and then, almost in slow motion, stumbled towards Byres Road, where he fell into the arms of a passer-by. The bystander placed him gently on the ground, with his back resting against an electricity junction box. Within seconds, he died.

In the meantime, Biswas turned his attention back to his wife, who was now in a sitting position on the pavement, supported by the railings. Biswas stood in front of her and took careful aim at her head. He pulled the trigger, but no shot rang out. He repeatedly tried to fire the pistol, but nothing happened. By now a number of onlookers were cautiously approaching the scene. Biswas turned and ran into the close, which allowed some brave passers-by to offer Alma Biswas some assistance. Within seconds, Biswas re-emerged from the close and confronted his wife's helpers. Biswas levelled his weapon at one particular individual, Eric Martin, and screamed at him, 'Get back. Get back or I'll shoot.' As Biswas moved the aim of his pistol over the five or six people who were assisting his wife, his expression was described as 'vacant and wild looking'.

One passer-by, Mrs McGill, who ran to the aid of Mrs Biswas, later stated to reporters that as she was bending over the injured wife just outside the close, Biswas re-appeared from inside the close and approached his wife. He took careful aim with his pistol and fired one shot into her prone body. Fearing more shots, Mrs McGill diver for cover but was surprised to see Biswas run back into the close mouth. Another witness, who was tending Mrs Biswas, stated that her husband attempted to shoot two more shots into his wife but the pistol misfired. It was then that he turned on his heels and ran into the close.

Leslie Johnston, a second-floor resident of 1 Lawrence Street, had heard the commotion, left his home and was coming down the stairs when he was barged out of the way by Biswas, who was on his way up. As he gathered himself, Johnston saw Biswas enter the open door of the Millar house and slam it shut behind him. Almost immediately after this, the sound of a gunshot was heard, quickly followed by another. Silence settled on the scene, but only for a few seconds, as another pistol crack echoed out of the house.

Two policemen, who had been walking in University Avenue, which is directly opposite Lawrence Street, had heard the first one or two shots and had come running to the scene. By the time of their arrival, Biswas was already within the Millar home and had fired three more shots. The officers ran upstairs but were met with a locked front door to the Millar flat. As they attempted to force it open, another shot rang out. The constables eventually broke open the front door and noticed a thin haze of gunsmoke filling the hallway of the flat. Both entered the first room on the left hand side and found Biswas sitting slumped in a chair.

His head was lying to one side and was covered in blood that oozed from a bullet wound to his head. Biswas' arm hung lifelessly over the side of the chair and his smoking automatic pistol lay on the carpet, inches below his outstretched fingers. It was quite obvious to the officers that Biswas was dead and they moved quickly to the next room along the hallway. Here they found the body of 60-year-old John Grant Millar, Biswas's father-in-law. The dead man was sitting in his chair at his desk, just in front of the window with a bullet wound dead centre in his forehead. Again, the officers entered the hallway and went to the room directly across the hallway, primarily because the door was slightly ajar. Just inside the room, they found a teenage girl lying on the floor. She had been shot once in the lower throat, just where it meets the chest. Blood saturated her light-coloured cotton dress and the floor surrounding her body. She was beyond help. She too was dead.

As the police examined her, they heard a baby crying. The officers turned their attention to a cot in the far corner of the room and were horrified to find nine-month-old Amal Biswas lying in a pool of blood. He had been shot once in the body but was still alive. Fortunately, other onlookers had already telephoned for further police assistance and ambulances to attend the scene. An ambulance arrived very quickly as the Western Infirmary was, (and still is), literally across the road from the location.

The child was removed first from the scene and taken to the infirmary but was pronounced dead on arrival. His little lungs had been punctured by the bullet and he had drowned in his own blood. Meanwhile, in another part of the hospital, doctors were working frantically on his mother, who was in a critical condition. The doctors faced a dilemma. The bullet fired into her body had struck a rib then ricocheted around her chest. The doctors wanted to remove the bullet, which had come to rest in her back, but had decided that Mrs Biswas was far too weak to undergo surgery of that magnitude.

The body of Thomas Strawbridge was also removed to the hospital but this was purely because it was lying out in the open. Once at the hospital, Strawbridge was formerly pronounced dead. The bodies of Mr Millar and his 14-year-old daughter Joan were quickly removed by ambulance wagon to the city mortuary. To avoid injuring any local feelings, another ambulance took Biswas' remains from the house to the same mortuary. Initial postmortem examinations on the bodies revealed that all had been killed by one shot each from a .25 automatic pistol. Fourteen cartridges of this calibre of ammunition had been found by police in a pocket of the jacket worn by Biswas.

Back at Lawrence Street, the police inquiry into the massacre had begun. Amid the confusion and panic that was sweeping through the district, the police were trying to calm fears of a public eager to hear the full story, by quickly establishing the facts of this shattering event. A reconstruction of the entire incident revealed the following catalogue of events. On the afternoon of the tragedy, Biswas visited his wife at Lawrence Street and the discussion turned to the divorce proceedings, which had been started the previous day. An argument developed between the couple which led to Biswas storming off about five pm. Where he went to, no one knows, but it was obviously to some place where he could uplift the gun he was to use to devastating effect later that evening.

It was just after 5.50pm when Biswas climbed into Strawbridge's cab at the taxi rank in Hope Street just outside Central Station and barked instructions that he should be taken to Lawrence Street. Alma Biswas was awaiting her estranged husband's arrival, possibly because during the earlier argument, he had threatened to return, but more likely because he had telephoned her to say that he was on his way. On seeing him arriving in a taxicab, Mrs Biswas darted from the house and down the stairs in an attempt to confront her husband in the street and keep him away from the family home, and more especially, her father.

Suffice to say that when he saw his wife approaching him, Biswas was so disturbed that he instantly fired a shot at her. The bullet struck her on the side of the head and, physically, completely stunned her. Blood gushed immediately from the wound and ran down her face. As she staggered, Thomas Strawbridge rushed across the street and Biswas turned his pistol on him. One shot straight into the heart stopped Strawbridge in his tracks. As people came forward, Biswas turned and fled into the close.

In the close, Biswas decided on his next action and exited from it. He found that his wife was already being assisted by various members of the public. However, he menaced and threatened Eric Martin before turning his gun towards his wife. Without hesitation, he shot her again. Not happy to leave it there, he tried twice more to shoot her but the gun either misfired, was empty or jammed. Once more, Biswas turned and ran into the close.

Police later discovered two unused bullets, one of which had a hammer indentation on its base, in the common close at the bottom of the stairway. This suggested to the police that Biswas' gun had misfired and then jammed, while the unused bullet may have been dropped by Biswas in his haste to reload his weapon. Biswas then climbed the stairs, pushing Leslie Johnston out of his way and entered the open door of the Millar's flat which had been left open by Mrs Biswas in her rush to confront her husband. He turned and locked the doors.

Biswas then entered the room that was used by Mr Millar in his daily business of being a dentist. As Mr Millar rose from his seated position at his desk to confront Biswas, he was shot once. The bullet entered his forehead, killing him instantly and he fell backwards into the chair. It is possible that Mr Millar had not heard any gunshots prior to being confronted by Biswas. This was because Millar's room windows looked out onto Byres Road, around the corner from where his daughter had been gunned down.

Biswas moved to the bedroom where his son slept. His 14-year-old sister-in-law, Joan, was comforting baby Amal when Biswas entered. As Joan placed the baby in the cot and turned to face Biswas, he shot her. The bullet hit her in the lower throat and threw her across the room, where she died moments later. Biswas then turned his attention to his son and fired a single shot into his son's body.

By this time, the police were trying to force entry to the main door of the flat. They could be clearly heard trying to kick in the door. Biswas entered the front room, used as a waiting room for the dental practice and moved an armchair into the centre of it. He sat down in the chair, facing the door he had just closed, placed the gun muzzle under his chin, and blew his brains out.

Mrs Biswas remained in a critical condition and was not fit enough to attend the funeral of her father, sister and young son, which took place on the afternoon of 16th August 1937, at the Western Necropolis in the north of the city, during one of the heaviest and prolonged rainstorms in years. All members of the public were barred from the cemetery until 15 minutes after the interment finished. Thereafter, what was described as 'a mad stampede' of over 2000 people, who crowded around the communal grave, eager to see the last resting place of the family who had been slaughtered by a madman.

In his life, Biswas had caused fury and upset and so it was in death also. His family, no doubt shocked and dismayed at what had occurred in Glasgow, became even more upset when they learned that Biswas' body had been cremated quietly and without any ceremony at Maryhill Crematorium on 17th August, the day after the family funeral. His ashes were thereafter scattered within the grounds of the crematorium, as per the wishes of the Millar family.

It was argued that, as a Hindu, this was against all of Biswas' religious beliefs and many disagreements between his family and friends arose with the authorities. However, most folk agreed that it had been done without any malice or intention to offend. The reality of the situation was that the authorities had volunteered to take care of all the arrangements for Biswas' funeral, as his family in India had not been in contact since being told of the outrage. However, Mrs Millar intimated her intention to make the arrange-ments, in conjunction with those of her own family's funeral.

The authorities made suggestions, which were followed by the Millar family; these were that Biswas's body should be cremated quietly and without fuss and his ashes scattered. This was simply to avoid any possibility of acts of retaliation by an outraged public. Without a grave, the population had no place to focus their anger.

Mrs Biswas eventually got stronger and an operation removed the bullet that was endangering her life. She left hospital a month after the bloodbath and returned to live with her mother and brothers at Lawrence Street. As is usual in circumstances such as this, Glaswegians raised a large amount of money by way of donations to a public appeal and generous pay outs were made to the Millar family and the disabled widow of Thomas Strawbridge. However, all too soon, the sad account of four murders and a suicide in a quiet Glasgow street on a sunny summer evening, faded from memory.

Chapter 14
Gorbals & Townhead, August 1938 & November 1945

The gas-lit streets and alleys of Glasgow's Gorbals were the breeding ground for the underbelly of society that was later to create its 'No Mean City' reputation. Patrick 'Paddy' Carraher had been born into a typical Gorbals family in 1907. He was schooled in the trades of thieving, fighting and drinking; skills and habits that were to last him a lifetime and ultimately cost him his life. His first brush with the law was in 1923 when he was arrested, charged and convicted of theft and assault. It was to be the start of a long relationship between Carraher and the authorities. By the late 1930s, with the Great Depression fading as quickly as Fascism was rising, Carraher had honed his skills to such a degree that he derived his entire income from crime. Indeed, with records being as hazy as they are, it is difficult to say if Carraher ever had a legitimate job at any time in his life.

On Saturday 13th August 1938, Paddy Carraher was standing on the pavement at Gorbals Cross, Glasgow. It was 11.15pm. As he stood there, drunk and swaying from side to side, he spotted a young girl nearby. Eighteen-year-old Margaret Nicol was waiting for her boyfriend to come along but before he did, Carraher sidled up to her and tried to strike up a conversation. From later statements, it would seem that Carraher was asking Nicol to act as a mediator between him and his then girlfriend, a Kate Morgan.

Nicol tried hard to ignore Carraher and frantically scanned all directions leading from Gorbals Cross, looking for her boyfriend. The minutes dragged out before a relieved Nicol spotted her saviour. She stepped down from the pavement and sprinted across the street and met up with James Durie, her 19-year-old beau. Carraher, in his drunken state, staggered after her, shouting and demanding that she co-operate with his wishes. Durie, shielding Nicol, threw in his opinions on the matter but before he finished his statement, Carraher grabbed him by the lapels of his jacket, pushed him back against the wall of the building and produced a knife which he held at Durie's throat. Whatever words were spoken at this time have not been recorded but when Carraher released his grip on Durie, the young man and his girlfriend ran off.

They didn't go too far. At 163 Hospital Street, they found Durie's elder brother, 24-year-old John, at home and they related their tale. Feeling aggrieved, the Durie brothers returned to the scene of the confrontation at Gorbals Cross. En route, they met up with 16-year-old Charlie Morgan, who was a brother-in-law of John Durie, and 23-year-old Peter Howard. Once there, Carraher was nowhere to be seen. So determined were they to confront Carraher, they hung around the area, looking for him. After half an hour, Carraher came lurching along the dark street. All four men barred his path and, never one to back down, Carraher began to argue with them.

It was later alleged that the Durie brothers were intent only on offering Carraher a 'fair fight' – one without weapons. Carraher may have been drunk but his instincts were still working. He refused the offer, saying that he was sure that the others would join in against him. As the noisy disagreement continued, it attracted the attention of another drunk who was making his way home. James Sydney Emden Shaw, a 23-year-old regular soldier, intervened and immediately rounded on Carraher. He told him that he 'sounded like an Englishman' and to 'shut up'. Carraher turned to face the intruder and they began trading insults. However, before matters got out of control, the beat policeman on patrol came upon the scene and warned all those present to behave themselves or face the consequences. In language they could clearly understand, he told everyone to 'take a walk'.

All of them began moving away from the Gorbals Cross area along nearby Ballater Street. The Durie brothers, along with Charlie Morgan, had had enough; the main argument had moved away from them and was now between Carraher and Shaw. As a result, the three relatives decided to go home. They left Howard to keep the peace between the two protagonists. Howard asked Shaw on two occasions if he would go home, to which the young soldier refused to agree, instead stating his intentions to stand his ground against Carraher. Having been rejected, Howard decided to leave them to it. Howard had walked no further than the breadth of the street when he turned to look back at the two men. What he saw was Shaw staggering into the roadway clutching his throat with blood spurting from between his fingers. Carraher was nowhere to be seen. As Howard went to help Shaw, the injured man ran off screaming along Ballater Street. After about 150 yards, he collapsed into the gutter. A crowd quickly gathered to assist the injured man and strenuous efforts were made to stem the heavy flow of blood from his neck. The policeman, who had only minutes earlier warned them all, arrived on the scene and immediately summoned an ambulance. Shaw died in it before it could reach the city's Royal Infirmary.

Two members of the crowd that had gathered around Shaw as he lay in the street were two 22-year-old girls – Mary McCafferty and Catherine Doherty. They saw the ambulance leave and then watched as Peter Howard was led into the rear of a police van. Concerned by this, the girls quickly made their way to the home of Robert Howard, Peter's brother, to tell him the news that a man had had his throat cut in Ballater Street and that Peter had been arrested. As they began their journey, they met with Carraher, lurking in the shadows and who was known to both of them. In their excited state, they blurted out what they had witnessed. All three went on to Howard's house and broke the news. Concerned for his brother's wellbeing, Robert Howard set off for the Central Police Station, accompanied by the girls and Carraher.

McCafferty and Carraher did not go all the way to the police station, instead stopping short at the Albert Bridge. The conversation between the pair centred on the incident and during this time, Carraher admitted to McCafferty that he was responsible. When she asked why he did it, Carraher's response was simply that Shaw 'had been cheeky to him'. Carraher then took from his jacket pocket a knife with a dark-coloured handle. He showed it to McCafferty and told her that was what he had used. Without any further conversation, Carraher threw the knife over the parapet of the bridge and into the waters of the River Clyde below.

In the police station, Robert Howard found out that his brother had not been arrested but had been taken to the police office to make a witness statement. With the matter having been clarified, Robert Howard and Doherty left the office, met up with the other two and headed off back to the Gorbals. Probably because Peter Howard hadn't been arrested, there was no further mention of Carraher's earlier boast to McCafferty that, 'they will let Peter out because I will give myself up: I won't let him swing for it.'

The following morning, Det Sgt John Johnstone along with other police officers, called at Carraher's home at 75 Florence Street. Carraher was lying in bed when he was formally cautioned and told of the reason for the early morning visit. 'Is he dead, right enough?' enquired Carraher. Without waiting for an answer, he then said, 'I was expecting this. I'll give you the full strength of it.' Carraher was taken into custody and remained there until his trial started on Monday, 12th September 1938.

A jury of nine women and six men listened to the evidence as it was presented by the prosecution. Medical evidence was led that showed that Shaw had been stabbed in the neck with a knife, severing his jugular vein. He bled to death. Police witnesses spoke of having measured the trail of blood in Ballater Street and calculated it at 136 yards in length. Two defence witnesses testified on Carraher's behalf. They told the court that they had been drinking with the accused man for most of that day and that he was so drunk he could hardly stand.

The trial went into its second day, during which closing arguments were heard. The judge, Lord Pitman, summarised the views and attempted to simplify matters. He explained that the law allowed a reduction of the murder charge to one of culpable homicide, a charge dependent on the state of mind of the person who had committed the act. Lord Pitman asked the jury to consider the level of provocation in the case, as this could also affect any possible verdict. The jury retired just after five minutes past one to consider their verdict and they remained in their room for two hours until the elected foreman asked if they could bring in a verdict of 'aggravated assault'.

Lord Pitman gave them the direction that if any person committed a serious assault that resulted in death, then that was culpable homicide. With that fresh information, the jury retired once more, this time for four minutes, and returned with a verdict of guilty of culpable homicide.

Carraher's counsel pleaded on his behalf for leniency, citing the fact he had only one previous conviction, which was, in a sense, true. He had only one previous conviction involving violence, although he had a great many more for dishonesty. Lord Pitman, in his sentencing speech to Carraher, stated, 'The jury have taken a lenient view of the case. I think their verdict means that they were satisfied you were under the influence of drink and had not the deliberate intent required in murder. Drinking can be found in a case of this kind to modify the conviction on the charge. Drinking is no excuse for assault which results in death. The crime of culpable homicide is very serious and the very least punishment I can inflict is penal servitude for three years.' Carraher was sent to jail and did his time without any notable incidents and was released in 1941, by which time, World War II was raging.

On his release, Carraher took up with a Sarah Bonnar and moved from the Gorbals to the Townhead area of the city. They set up home as man and wife at No 14 Tarbet Street; his common-law wife had a brother, Daniel Bonnar and both he and Carraher had a similar mentality; together they made a violent pair. In February 1943, the duo went on a drunken spree and began rampaging through the Townhead district; everyone they met was subjected to violence. This led to Bonnar being charged with assaulting a woman with a bottle while Carraher faced allegations that he threatened three women with an open razor and thereafter, in a local pub, attempted to slash a man with the same weapon. Fortunately for the intended victim, Carraher missed his target and instead ripped through the man's clothing. Nonetheless, the intent was present and at his trial on 11th May 1943, Carraher was found guilty of all the charges and received another three years in jail. Bonnar got 18 months.

This time, with a combination of good behaviour and the war coming to an end, Carraher was released early from his sentence in September 1945. As soon as he got out, he took up with Bonnar again. It was almost as if he had never been away. About 4.30pm on Friday 23rd November that year, three brothers, John, Joseph and Edward Gordon left their father's house in McAslin Street, Townhead. They had cause for celebration as John was on demob leave having just been released from a German POW camp. He had been captured just outside St Valery in the retreat to Dunkirk in 1940 while a member of the Seaforth Highlanders. All told, he had been a solider for 20 years.

The brothers' first port of call was to their sister's house, where they met with her husband, Duncan Revie. He was a deserter from the Royal Army Service Corps but that didn't stop the men from being friends. The four men went to the Coronation Bar further along McAslin Street and began drinking. About seven pm that night, the revellers decided to move on to another public house, Cameron's in nearby Rottenrow, and here they remained for the next two and a half hours until closing time. During this period, they were joined by another friend, John Keatings, who was a deserter from the Royal Navy. (It was estimated that in 1945-6, Glasgow had over 10,000 deserters from the armed forces living in the city. Rising crime rates were attributed to them and the problems became so bad that a special task force was set up in an attempt to rectify matters.) So good were the celebrations, the two youngest Gordons (Joseph and Edward) passed out in the pub due to the amount of alcohol they had drunk. From all accounts, the remaining three were just on the right side of consciousness.

Just a little bit further along the street from Cameron's was another pub, Thompson's. Paddy Carraher and Daniel Bonnar had been drinking in there all day and most of the evening, only leaving around 8.15pm when they decided to have a party in Bonnar's house. They invited along a number of their drinking companions. By 9.30pm, as all the public houses in the area disgorged themselves of their patrons, the alcohol was running low at the party in Bonnar's house. As host, Bonnar volunteered to go and get more to drink and to find others to join in the fun. As he tried to force his way past those milling around outside Cameron's bar, Bonnar came face to face with

John Gordon, Revie and Keatings. There was no initial problem but then Keatings, in a very loud voice, offered the advice that he was about to clear the street of those he considered inferior to himself.

No one, apart from Bonnar, took much notice of Keatings' drunken boastfulness. Taking up the challenge, Bonnar stepped forward and removed his jacket, folding it neatly before carefully placing it on the pavement next to a lamppost. Without any further ceremony, both men began fighting. Irrespective of who was winning or losing, Revie decided to help out Keatings and both men got on to Bonnar. The challenger didn't wait around long enough to get hurt and ran off, chased by Keatings. Bonnar reached the sanctity of a sister's house in nearby College Street and once sufficiently recovered, borrowed his sister's jacket and a hatchet. He decided to return to the area of the public house and exact his revenge.

Unbeknown to Bonnar, his flight from conflict was observed by a neighbour, Mrs Helen Colquhoun, who felt it was her civic duty to go to the party house and inform Carraher and others of what she had seen. Armed with this information, Carraher and another partygoer, Thomas Connelly Watt left the flat and went looking for their friend. They soon found him, probably because he was hard to miss, wearing, as he was, a brightly coloured ladies jacket and carrying an axe!

All three began searching for those who had accosted Bonnar. On the corner of McAslin Street and Taylor Street, they found their quarry. Revie was helping John Gordon along the road, such was his drunken condition, when they were ambushed by Carraher, Bonnar and Watt. Bonnar swung the hatchet at Revie's head, striking him with the reverse edge but then once more, took fright, turned and ran off. Revie chased after him, with Watt bringing up the rear. Gordon, totally oblivious to all that had gone on, stood holding onto a lamppost, trying to keep his balance.

Carraher, with a weapon in his hand, came up behind Gordon and struck him one blow to the rear of his neck. Gordon fell off the edge of the pavement and into the roadway, where he lay until assisted by about four or five members of the public. They managed, rightly or wrongly, to get him back to his feet and had helped him only a short distance when a breathless Revie arrived back on the scene. He quickly threw Gordon over his shoulder and carried him to the close mouth of his own house. With Gordon in a very bad way, a taxi was found and the injured man was taken the short distance to the Royal Infirmary. The duty doctor examined Gordon at the gatehouse and authorised his immediate admission. The injured man died on the stretcher, one minute after the examination.

Word quickly spread around Townhead that murder had been committed. One who couldn't wait to tell his piece of news was taxi driver, 27-year-old John Stewart, who called at Carraher's flat. He took the news quietly whilst Bonnar was highly excited. At one point, Bonnar was heard to say, 'It's alright. I will take the consequences.' Perhaps Carraher sensed future problems, for he took Stewart into another room and told him that he had given Gordon 'a jag'. He then produced a wooden-handled chisel, wiped it with a dishcloth and then snapped it into two pieces, handed them both to Stewart and said, 'Chip them away.' When Stewart left Carraher's house minutes later, the first thing he did was to drop the chisel down a road drain. The handle part couldn't be forced through the grid covering the drain and had to be dropped down another, larger drain cover further along the street.

Later that morning, Carraher's flat was raided by a swarm of police officers, some uniformed and some not. He, Bonnar and Watt were arrested and subsequently remanded in custody, charged with the murder of John Gordon. Revie was also arrested and charged separately with a breach of the peace. He pled guilty at his first court appearance and was sentenced to six months' imprisonment. He was still serving that sentence when he was summoned to the High Court in Glasgow to give evidence against Carraher, whose trial for the murder of John Gordon began on 28th February 1946. Both Bonnar and Watt had the murder charge against them dropped when the full details of that November night fracas became clear.

Bonnar actually raised ripples of laughter in the midst of the solemn proceedings of the courtroom when he tried to explain that, dressed in a woman's jacket that was at least four sizes too small for him, his intention was to confront Revie and Gordon and 'get the thing fixed without a fight.' The next time Bonnar spoke in court was to agree with the suggestion that he did all this while concealing an axe up the sleeve of the aforementioned jacket and thereafter using it to strike Revie on the head!

The defence case was centred on three examinations of Carraher, carried out by two eminent psychiatrists. The doctors' diagnosis was that Carraher's attitude was abnormal and he did not seem to appreciate the seriousness of the matter now at hand. He also displayed 'a gross lack of moral sense and social responsibility'. All in all, his manner seemed to be one of nonchalance. Damningly for the defence, both doctors considered that Carraher, for all his mental shortcomings, was sane and fit to stand trial.

By Saturday morning, 2nd March, and with all arguments and summing up finished, the jury of nine men and six women trooped out of the courtroom to go and deliberate the facts of the case. Twenty minutes later they returned with a unanimous verdict of guilty. Lord Russell had no option but to pass the death sentence and he set the date of execution for 23rd March at Barlinnie Prison.

Within a week of the end of the trial, Carraher's defence team had lodged an appeal on two counts. First, that the court should have had an appointed psychiatric assessor and second, that the judge had misdirected the jury regarding evidence of Carraher's identification.

On Wednesday 20th March, the Court of Appeal in Edinburgh dismissed the appeal. Carraher had been present throughout the appeal court hearing until it came time to announce the five judges' decision. He did not appear in court to hear the outcome, being told the news in a side room instead. Carraher was then driven back to Barlinnie Prison. As a result of the appeal process, the execution was rescheduled for 6th April. On Wednesday 27th March, a petition bearing a small number of signatures was handed into the Scottish Office in Edinburgh, asking that Carraher be reprieved. It failed.

On Saturday 6th April 1946, just before eight am, Patrick 'Paddy' Carraher found himself standing on the scaffold within Barlinnie Prison. Unlike his victims, he didn't feel anything sharp against his neck; a good stiff rope saw to that.

Chapter 15
Anniesland, March 1942

Today, Anniesland Cross, in the city's West End, is one of the major road junctions in Glasgow. It is also recognised as one of the largest in Europe and as one of the most complicated, in terms of the number of traffic lights which numbered over 50 at the last count. So it can be safely stated that for 24 hours a day, seven days a weeks, something is always happening at this location. The Pilkington's glass factory on the north side employed so many workers that the streets around it were described as 'awash with people' when they decanted from the works at the end of the working day (this site is now a Morrison's supermarket). It was no different during the years of World War II. Not only was it a traffic junction but it had housing and businesses at every turn. It had shops on the eastern side of the junction on Great Western Road for as long as anyone can remember and still has. A newsagent, a green-grocer, a tailor and a bank were amongst the 20 or so shops that operated in the vicinity in those days. One particular shop, at 1595 Great Western Road, was smaller than all the others. But the size of the shop was just right for 55-year-old Reginald Sanderson, who ran his watchmaker and jewellery business from it. The shop had a window display area and a workshop in the rear and it provided a comfortable living for Sanderson and his wife.

On Saturday 14th March 1942, Sanderson opened his shop for business at the usual time of nine am. He had been on the premises all night, doing his duty as a firewatcher, acting as a lookout in case the Luftwaffe bombed Glasgow during the night. The morning went as normal and about 10.45 he decided to close the shop and go to his home at 11 Strathcona Street, which was nearby, to check on his wife who was an invalid. He locked up the premises and placed a small envelope in the window of the door. The handwritten message on it read: 'Back at 11.30'. The card was seen by a couple of potential customers but no one thought of it as out of the ordinary. Sure enough, Mr Sanderson arrived back at his shop at the specified time and found a customer waiting in the doorway for him.

As the morning progressed, Sanderson dealt with a trickle of customers. About 1.30pm a customer called at the shop and found another sign on the door: 'Gone for Lunch – back at 1.30'. As it was that time, the customer tried the door and found it open. He entered the shop but there was no one behind the counter and no one answered when he called out on two or three occasions. The customer leaned over the counter in order to try to look into the rear of the shop and was horrified to see a trail of blood on the floor. The customer slowly moved towards the rear of the shop and quickly found Mr Sanderson lying on the floor in a recessed part of the back of the shop which was used as a workroom. Sanderson was lying on his side and his feet and hands were bound with black cord. Closer inspection revealed that one of his hands had come free from the binding and that a scarf or towel had been tied around the lower part of his face, covering his mouth. Blood was everywhere in the workshop and Mr Sanderson was obviously dead. The customer had seen enough, ran out of the shop and went next door to summon the police.

The police arrived and immediately began murder investigations. They closely examined the shop premises. A full forensic examination was carried out and both back and front shops were thoroughly inspected for any finger-print evidence. At first, robbery did not seem to be a motive for Sanderson's murder. His body was found to have a wallet in a pocket which had over £60 in notes in it. Another wallet was found on a shelf in the workshop and had £23 10s in it. The shop till was found to be intact and contained £5. While the front shop appeared in its usual condition, the rear shop was in quite a mess and looked to some as if it might have been ransacked.

The police found a garden spade in the back shop, which they thought was out of place for a jeweller's shop. It was quickly explained that the previous week, when Glasgow was hit with a late-winter attack of heavy snowfall, Sanderson had purchased the spade to clear snow from the front of his shop. Nonetheless, police examined it and discovered that it was, in fact, the probable murder weapon. Blood and hairs were smeared all over it. It was difficult for police to tell if anything had been stolen, so one of the first things police did was to appeal for customers to come forward and tell them of their dealings with the jeweller.

Over the remainder of the weekend, police remained in the shop and a number of customers actually called there and gave statements as to their business dealings with Mr Sanderson. The police had a major difficulty in understanding how those responsible could carry out the crime and then exit from the shop, probably tainted with blood, into one of the busiest streets in Glasgow and at one of the busiest times of the day, without being seen by anyone. They appealed for all bus, tram drivers and conductors to report any suspicious passengers. Police were also working on theories as to how the crime unfolded. They speculated that Sanderson was serving a customer or customers when he had occasion to go through to the rear workshop area. Another possibility is that he was forced into this area by his killer or killers.

Once in the workshop, Sanderson was struck a blow which knocked him to the floor and rendered him temporarily senseless. He was then tied up by his hands and feet and gagged with a duster from the shop. The shop was then ransacked but many valuables were ignored. At some point during the attack, Mr Sanderson managed to free his right hand from his bindings and partially removed the gag from his mouth. It would appear that whoever was attacking him panicked and began hitting the elderly shopkeeper with the garden spade that was lying against a wall in the workshop. Sanderson was so severely beaten about the head and face that he succumbed to the attack and died.

A later postmortem revealed that Reginald Sanderson's skull had been smashed; he was so severely beaten that pieces of brain matter were found mixed in with the blood spatter that had adhered to the walls of the workshop. The pathologist also stated that all of the blows had been delivered with the flat surface of the spade and not with the sharp edge. These facts – using cord, a duster and a spade, which all belonged to the shop – suggested to police that the crime had been spur-of-the-moment and was not premeditated. While police tried to figure out how the crime happened, they expressed their concern that some members of the public held vital information but were still not coming forward; people in the district had been reluctant to talk to police.

By the end of the weekend, police had narrowed down the time of the murder. It was known that Mr Sanderson had served a female customer about 12.10pm and he seemed his usual self. About 1.05pm another customer called at the shop and noticed the 'Gone to Lunch' sign in the door window. However, he tried the door and found it open. The customer entered but there was no one in the front shop. He knocked loudly on the shop counter and even shouted, trying to attract attention, but he got no reply. He thought that Mr Sanderson had simply forgotten to lock the door and he left, pulling the door firmly behind him. Another customer found the body about 25 minutes later.

By the middle of the following week, police were reportedly complaining that they had received quite a number of anonymous letters. While some of them contained potential leads, the police needed to ask questions of the letter writers but could not do so due to their anonymity. One such letter in particular perplexed them. It came from a woman and in it she related a

105

conversation she had had with a female friend, who she also failed to identify. This friend of the writer alleged that she had seen two uniformed soldiers entering Sanderson's shop on the Saturday in question at lunchtime. When the letter writer advised her friend to go to the police, she was told, 'No fear. I don't want to be mixed up in it.' The police appealed for this particular letter writer to get back in touch, explaining that 'she may be the means of solving this mystery.'

The police also spent a number of days and a great number of man-hours investigating Sanderson's links with greyhound racing. It appeared that this was a particular hobby of his and he was a well-kent face at dog tracks across the city. The suggestion was that the money in his wallet, missed by his killer(s), was his winnings. All of his racing acquaintances were interviewed, to discover if any of them held a grudge against Sanderson or to uncover if he had any enemies.

A week after the murder, police got a major breakthrough in the case when they received information as to the identity of a possible suspect. An aircraftman, based at an RAF station in England, was reported to have tried to get his uniform cleaned but parts of it were found to be saturated in blood. This had raised suspicions and the police were notified. As a result, two senior detectives were despatched to an unnamed RAF base in England, where they interviewed the serviceman. At the end of the interview, the detectives arrested the man and made arrangements to transport him back to Glasgow to face court. George Henry Price, a 21-year-old member of the RAF, appeared at Glasgow Marine Police Court on Wednesday 25th March. He was wearing full uniform. Price was formally charged with the murder of Reginald Sanderson and of robbing him of five finger rings, a watch, a brooch, a diamante clip and 10 shillings in money. He was kept in custody pending further inquiries and eventually remanded until the date of his trial. Prior to this, at a pleading diet at Glasgow Sheriff Court on 6th June, Price's solicitor lodged a special plea in bar of trial in that Price was insane at the time of the murder, and further, that he was insane at present. The case was continued to the High Court.

On Tuesday, 16th June 1942, Price appeared in the dock of Glasgow's High Court of Justiciary, again in full RAF uniform. Immediately, the matter of his special plea of insanity was dealt with. The judge, Lord Justice-Clerk, Lord Cooper listened intently as medical evidence was led. Dr George Scott, medical officer at Barlinnie Prison was first to give his opinion. Price had been under his constant observation during his remand in the prison, during which period he had been interviewed and examined on several occasions too. It is known that he was born in Glasgow in 1920 and that he was a lone child. His mother resided in Glasgow and had visited him during his detention on remand. The facts that emerged were that no one in his family had any history of mental disorder. His behaviour throughout his early years was classed as totally unacceptable and when he was 12 years old, he ran away from home. During his time 'on the run', he stole a number of items from a shop, was caught and sent to an approved school until he was 16 years old. Having been released he managed to secure himself a job as an apprentice in the Govan shipyards but that didn't last long. He then managed to find a job in a cinema but he didn't survive in that job for any length of time either. For the next couple of years, Price flitted from one job to another, never remaining in any of them for more than two months at a time.

In June 1939, Price's behaviour was such that he was classed as clinically insane and was incarcerated in Glasgow Royal Mental Hospital at Gartnavel for six months. When released in December, and with World War II just getting underway, he immediately joined the RAF and began life as an aircraftman. However, even in the services, his bad behaviour continued and he got himself into trouble regularly with authority. Price was physically fit but was a persistent liar and thief. He frequently committed crimes and he was unable to resist criminal impulses. He felt no shame or remorse for any of his actions and would vehemently deny any involvement, even in the face of overwhelming evidence to the contrary. Price was totally incapable of determining right from wrong or the consequences of his behaviour. Two further doctors, Dr Ivy McKenzie and Dr Angus McNiven, gave evidence of a similar nature. Lord Cooper had little alternative but to agree with the medical opinion and decreed that Price was insane and unable to stand trial. He ordered that Price would be detained during His Majesty's pleasure.

It is strange that police were able to visit an RAF base in the middle of England and arrest the man who had committed the crime. The truth of the matter is quite sensational. Quite simply, Price had written to the police and confessed to the murder.

In most murder cases, especially if the case is given significant publicity, much correspondence will be received by police from many varied sources. Some of these letters will contain claims of the writer's involvement in the murder. Normally, after being read, they are ignored. However, Price's letter contained sufficient detailed knowledge of the crime to alert the police. Some of the details described by him in his letter had not been made public. The newspapers of the day didn't pay any extra attention to the case. Newsprint was severely limited due to the war and most daily papers were restricted to around 10 pages per issue. There was much war news that needed to be reported and therefore very little room for local stories. The murder of Reginald Sanderson, and the subsequent arrest and detention of George Henry Price, fought for space with headlines about the fighting in Bataan, the raid on the docks at St Nazaire and speculation about the whereabouts of the German battleship *Tirpitz*.

A number of unusual points came to the fore in this case. The fact that Price wrote a letter to police admitting his guilt seems to contradict what all the doctors said when they advised that Price never owned up to his criminal actions. However, a letter was received, which contained 'specialist knowledge', and that led police to interview Price. Another anomaly was that Price appeared in court on more than one occasion and was described as wearing the uniform of an officer of the RAF. The reality was that Price was not an officer in the RAF for a number of very good reasons; one of the best of which was that he had been in trouble constantly during his service, so much so that the RAF were probably glad to see the back of him when the police arrested him. Price wore a uniform to which he had no entitlement and the authorities seem to have tolerated this continued charade for some unknown reason. It is possible that it was part of Price's insanity.

George Henry Price remained a mystery man for most of his life. Very little information about him escaped into the public domain. There is no record of his release from detention.

Chapter 16
Pollokshields, December 1945

The freezing fog that enveloped Glasgow on the dark and cold winter
night of 10th December 1945, was affectionately called 'a pea-souper'. It
deadened all noise and cast unusual, almost eerie, shadows. One particularly
dense bank of mist had settled over the small railway station of Pollokshields
East on the Cathcart Line on the south side of the city. The intensity of the
fog was multiplied by a peculiarity of the station in that it lay quite a distance
below the level of the surrounding streets. Not surprisingly, all trains were
running late because of the foul weather. This meant that the staff of the little
station had about 20 minutes to spare before the next train was due to arrive.

Just after 7.30pm William Wright, the 42-year-old porter/clerk, Annie
Withers, the station clerkess and 15-year-old junior porter, Robert Gough,
found themselves in the stationmaster's office, trying to warm up in front of
the small coal fire in a corner of the room. As they sat there the silence was
broken by the office door being kicked open. In the space stood a male with
a gun in his hand. The three railway workers were frozen in horror at what
confronted them. The gunman was the only one to speak. 'This is a hold-
up', he growled. A piercing scream echoed around the small room. It was
Annie Withers. She never got to finish as the pistol exploded in the gunman's
hand. The bullet struck Withers in her left arm, passed completely through,
then entered her left thigh. The force of it all threw her back against the wall.
Young Gough stooped across to help her, and the gun barked once more.
The bullet buried itself in his stomach.

Wright was rooted to the spot but the gunman turned his attention on
him. One shot was enough. Wright felt the pain in his side and fell to the
floor, landing on top of Gough. The gunman wasn't finished. Annie Withers
was still screaming. He coolly stepped forward, bringing himself further into
the office and fired his pistol twice more. Both shots were aimed at the
terrified clerkess and they found flesh, one in her chest and the other in her
stomach. Withers slid slowly down the wall, silently. From first shot to last,
no more than ten seconds had elapsed. The gunman disappeared from the
doorway as quickly as he had appeared.

Wright was not too badly injured, the bullet having passed through his outer clothing and grazing his skin on the right hand side of his chest. However, in the silence of the room, he could hear the gunman in the booking office next door. Fearing that he might come back and finish him off, he lay completely motionless on the floor. Wright distinctly heard the opening of the drawer in the safe that was in the office, but it was only when he heard the sound of the outer door of the office slam shut that he dared to move. He got to his feet and staggered through the adjoining doorway into the booking office. From there, he used the telephone to call the signalman at the nearby junction signal box. Wright pleaded with the signalman to get help quickly.

Wright then went back into the stationmaster's office and tried to lift Annie Withers off the floor as the blood oozed slowly from her wounds. His intention was to try to make her comfortable by sitting her upright in a chair. He only succeeded in causing her more pain, which in turn caused her to moan loudly, and he quickly gave up on that idea. By this time, Wright could hear a train approaching the station. He began to stagger towards the platform and reached it only to find the disembarked passengers disappearing up the stairs and the guard on the train about to signal the driver to depart. Wright blurted out what had happened and the unbelievable occurred. The guard thought it was all a joke, blew his whistle for the train to start, and as it began moving off, jumped aboard without even another glance at Wright, who had dropped to his knees on the platform.

When Wright turned round to go back into the offices, he found that young Gough had crawled out of the room onto the platform and somehow or other, managed to haul himself onto a station bench. Gough lay there, writhing in pain, and Wright went towards him to offer some comfort. A few minutes later, two policemen who had been summoned by the signalbox man came running down the stair from the street above. The officers were closely followed by a number of other railway workers, alerted by the same source.

Ambulances were called to the scene and all the injured parties were taken to the Victoria Infirmary. Annie Withers was found to be dead on arrival, her injuries too massive for her to survive. Robert Gough, although young, fit and strong, also succumbed to his wounds after two days of intensive treatment. Before he died, he was able to provide the authorities, in the shape of Sheriff-Substitute Arthur Gillies, with a dying deposition.

The entire station was sealed off. Trains were not permitted to stop whilst the investigations were ongoing. Specialist officers were called in and they managed to obtain a number of fingerprint impressions from the drawers of the safe. A check revealed that the only thing missing from the safe was a brown envelope containing a local signalman's weekly wages – £4 3s 8d. (£4.19). Wright was interviewed at length and was able to give a description of the gunman, which was as follows; about 30 years of age, 5ft 8in-10in tall, wearing a light-coloured raincoat and a black soft hat, which had been pulled down tight, almost covering his eyes. Young Gough had given a very similar description but was able to add that the gunman had short red or ginger-coloured hair. The police quickly discovered that the weapon used had been a 9mm Luger pistol, but when they tried to match the fingerprints they had obtained to those in their records, they failed to find a match. There were no other witnesses to the double murder.

The Scottish *Daily Express* newspaper offered a £1,000 reward for information leading to an arrest, but even so, the police enquiry gradually ground to a halt. Eventually, even the newspapers lost interest in the story and it disappeared from their pages, replaced by news of events in Europe and Japan. However, the police continued to investigate every lead that came their way. They followed up on men fitting the description or of someone talking in a pub about the killings. Unfortunately, all their enquiries came to nothing.

On 8th October 1946, two detectives were assigned the task of following up on a snippet of anonymous information that suggested a man who resided in the area of the robbery was the owner of a Luger-type pistol. The detectives called at the address only to find that the man in question was out at work. He had a job as a railway fireman and on this particular day, was working on a long-distance engine. His mother expected him home early next morning. The officers left a message, asking that he attend at the local police office the following day.

The next morning, just before 10am, Constable John Byrne was on traffic point duty in Spean Street, Glasgow, when he was approached by 21-year-old Charles Templeman Brown, who asked, without any formalities, 'Will you phone Central for me?'. 'Why?' asked the officer, to which Brown replied casually, 'I did a murder. The Pollokshields job.' Although initially taken aback at the startling admission, Byrne recovered sufficiently to take Brown into custody and march him to a nearby police box, from where he telephoned his office for assistance. While waiting for reinforcements to arrive, Byrne searched Brown and took from him a 1918 model Luger pistol and a box of ammunition.

Brown's confession and arrest caused quite a ripple of excitement in both the police and, eventually, the newspapers. His home was searched and among the many items taken for further investigation was a pistol holster. Later that day, Brown was placed on an identification parade and, although it was now ten months since the tragic events, William Wright was immediately able to identify Brown in the line-up of 12 men.

Although he had confessed to the murders, the police still had a job to do collecting the evidence. The Luger pistol was tested and the bullets compared to those used to kill both Withers and Gough. They were found to match perfectly. Brown's fingerprints were also taken and compared to the impressions lifted from the station safe. Again, they matched. He was remanded in custody to Barlinnie Prison to await trial.

By a strange quirk of fate Brown's trial opened at Glasgow's High Court on 10th December 1946, exactly one year after the events of that murderous, foggy day. While the case against Brown appeared to be overwhelming, he pled not guilty to all the charges. The prosecution led their witnesses, including William Wright and all the pertinent evidence involving the gun, fingerprints and confession. One important witness for the Crown, Det Sgt Murdoch McKenzie, told the court that Brown had said to him at the time of his arrest, 'I would be walking about dressed today if yon wee boy had not dived at me. I didn't mean to kill anybody, but once you start shooting, you can't stop.' Brown was referring to Robert Gough, the boy porter, and trying to offer some mitigation for his murderous behaviour that night. According to Gough's dying deposition, the reality was that the young lad didn't dive at Brown but was instead trying to use his body to protect Annie Withers from further gunshots.

Brown sat impassively in the dock. Not one piece of incriminating information heard by the court seemed to disturb him. To those who witnessed the trial, it appeared that Brown was in another world. Hector Murray, a 24-year-old student friend of Brown's, told the court that the accused had a fascination with Frank Sinatra in as much as Brown dressed similarly to Sinatra and on occasions would play the singer's records all day. Later in the trial, Brown's mother gave evidence that her son had once travelled all the way to London in order to buy a jacket similar to one worn by Sinatra. His mother also stated that Brown had a fascination with both Hitler and Stalin, adorning his bedroom walls with their pictures.

Somewhat surprisingly, Mrs Brown also stated that her son was a devout fan of the bandleader, Joe Loss. Even the most naive of laymen would have to agree that Brown's fixations were bizarrely diverse. The first medical evidence came from a Dr Blyth. He was of the opinion that Brown was suffering from a disease known as incipient dementia praecox, more commonly known today as schizophrenia. In 1948, dementia praecox was a disease of which the causes were unknown. What was known was that it could manifest itself in the patient as a desire for publicity. The patient would also visualise himself as a hero in his world of daydreams. However, if Brown did suffer from it, Dr Blyth stated that while medically he considered the accused insane, legally he was not. Two more doctors with opinions were called to enhance the defence case. However, their views were similar to those of Dr Blyth.

On the third day of the trial, the jury was subjected to the final submissions from both the Crown and the defence teams. The judge, Lord Carmont, also summed up. He was at pains to point out to the jury what may have been the most important statement made during those three days. He said that while there is a presumption of innocence for the accused, there was also a presumption of sanity. It was therefore, the defence's job to prove the case for insanity, or as they had suggested during the trial, diminished responsibility.

The jury took just over an hour to reach their verdict. Brown stood motionless as the majority decision was delivered – guilty of murder. Lord Carmont produced the black cap and it was placed on top of his wig. He then passed the death sentence on Brown, who still looked totally unmoved. Execution was arranged for 3rd January 1947. Once again an appeal was lodged with the authorities and on 31st December 1946, four days before Brown's appointment with his fate, he learned that he was to be spared the hangman's noose and a term of life imprisonment was imposed instead.

However, the story of Charles Templeman Brown does not end there, with him left to spend the remainder of his life in prison. He served ten years in jail, was released in 1957 and set up as a travelling salesman with a firm of tyre manufacturers based in Glasgow. One winter's night, he was driving a hired car on the A9 Glasgow to Perth road when, just outside Dunblane, the vehicle failed to take a bend, shot off the road, crashed through a wall and came to rest in a ditch.

The female passenger was badly injured, but Brown was killed instantly. The date was 10th December 1960, the 13th anniversary of the railway shootings. It was the third time this date had featured in Brown's life, once again with fatal consequences.

Chapter 17
Washington Street, October 1945

At the turn of 1945, Glasgow was bursting at the seams with returning servicemen, happy to be demobbed and coming home to their families. As stated elsewhere in this book, approximately 10,000 deserters were thought to have been hiding out in the city; Glasgow at the end of World War II really was teeming with life. What was also in abundance were illicit weapons; all types of guns and knives had been brought back in kitbags, mostly as innocent mementos, but some for a more sinister intent. As the soaring crime rates of the late 1940s and early 1950s now show, these weapons were not just for decoration or display purposes. They were to be used.

Some of the younger male population of the city, who had not been old enough to see any wartime action, seemed intent on exercising feelings of tribal anger and territorial dominance and had formed themselves into gangs with other like-minded individuals. Glasgow has always had gangs but it appeared that during times of world conflict, the gangs at home flourished. Some returning servicemen were keen to perpetuate their fighting mentality and many joined their local gang. What they brought to the gangs was illicit weapons and the mindset and ability to use them. The violence levels during confrontations between rival gangs increased dramatically. Newspapers were filled on an almost daily basis with stories of all manner of serious violent crime involving young men armed with knives or similar.

John Thomas Brady was 19 years of age and had, on Monday 15th October 1945, been demobilised from the Royal Navy and returned to his home at 77 Carrick Street in the Anderston area of the city for the first time in over a year. He spent the first few days getting re-acquainted with his friends and catching up on all the local news. Very quickly, he slotted back into his old routine. On Saturday, 20th October, he decided to go to a senior football match in the afternoon and when it had finished, he returned home about five pm. His mother served him his evening meal and he then spent the next hour or so readying himself for a night out with his girlfriend. Brady took her to a dance hall in the East End of the city and on their return they caught a tramcar for home. During the journey, Brady had a chance meeting with his sister and her husband who had been attending a city-centre cinema. All four alighted from the tramcar in Argyle Street as it passed Carrick Street.

As soon as they got off the tramcar, Brady was met by his mother, who had been standing on the street corner, talking to a friend. She told her son that there had been quite a disturbance just a short time before his arrival and that was why the district was busier than normal. A gang of armed men had rampaged along Brown Street and Carrick Street, chasing any young men who were unfortunate enough to be seen by them. Knives, bayonets, large sticks and even a firearm had all been brandished. Joseph Patrick Smyth, also 19, was a member of a gang called the 'Dougie Boys', named after nearby Douglas Street. He had been standing on the corner of Douglas Street and Argyle Street, about 10.20pm, talking to a couple of girls, when he saw a large group of youths coming along Argyle Street. He could hear them shouting, 'Where are the Dougie Boys?' and 'We are the Crosbies.'

The group of youths spotted Smyth and began to cross Argyle Street in his direction. Smyth, seeing that some of the group were carrying weapons, immediately made a run for it and jumped onto the platform of a passing tramcar. He saw two of the group break off and make towards the tram in an effort to intercept him. No sooner had Smyth got on the tram when he jumped off and ran around the front of the vehicle, attempting to hide from them. By now, others in the group of youths were approaching him and he took to his heels down nearby Brown Street. The group of youths reformed, and as one, began running down the centre of the roadway, chasing after Smyth.

Mr and Mrs Macklin, of 26 Brown Street, gave statements later saying that they were standing at their close mouth when Smyth ran past them quickly. They said that all of the pursuing youths were brandishing a weapon of some sort, mostly knives and bayonets. One youth held aloft a small revolver, although it wasn't fired. They could clearly hear the group shouting various slogans, including a crude version of 'If anybody wants it, they can get it.'

On hearing all of this, John Brady felt highly aggrieved at another gang invading 'Dougie Boy' territory. He, along with a number of other youths, began to actively seek a confrontation with the intruders in order to restore some misguided sense of respect and principle. As 22-year-old John McFarlane of St Vincent Street was later heard to say, 'I followed them because I thought there was going to be a fight. If there was going to be one, I wanted to be in it.' What happened next has been described by many witnesses, many of whom did not see all of the incident but only certain parts of it, because it took place over a number of different streets. By piecing together the various accounts, a full picture of events can be obtained.

John Brady and about five or six others, all members of the 'Dougie Boys', gathered together on the corner of Crimea Street and Carrick Street. Their intention was to confront the rival group of youths who had earlier chased one of their number. Word soon reached them that the group they were after was currently in the Broomielaw and heading westwards. The 'Dougie Boys' decided to intercept them and, by using shortcuts through closes and backcourts, very quickly found themselves in Washington Street.

As Brady and the rest of the 'Dougie Boys' ran down Washington Street, towards the Broomielaw, they were themselves confronted by their quarry at the foot of the street. For the 'Dougie Boys', this was their desired intention. However, what they didn't bank on was being outnumbered by almost two to one. Within seconds of meeting, more and more youths joined the other group, whose numbers increased to about 15. Some of them were openly carrying their weapons. Feeling vulnerable at this point, the 'Dougie Boys', as one, turned and ran back up Washington Street, their only escape route.

What was in the 'Dougie Boys' favour was that they were local and knew their territory; they knew the correct closes to run into to give them a better chance of escape. And that is exactly what happened. One or two of those being pursued darted into closes and dodged into backcourts. Only a couple of the chasing gang broke off the pursuit to follow them. The remaining visiting gang members stopped running when they reached the corner of Balaclava Street. One of the 'Dougie Boys', in trying to turn the corner of the tenement building, slipped and fell on the pavement. It was John Thomas Brady.

Other members of the 'Dougie Boys' kept running but after another hundred yards or so, they realised that they had lost their leader and that they were no longer being pursued. They stopped running and looked back to see what had happened. From witness statements, as soon as Brady had fallen, he was surrounded by the chasing gang and it was visibly obvious that knives and bayonets were being used to assault the youth. After a minute or so, the visiting gang stopped the assault and began walking off towards nearby Argyle Street.

As the gang dispersed, it was seen that Brady was lying on his back on the pavement, motionless. His 17-year-old brother, Joseph, who had been one of the fleeing 'Dougie Boys', began to approach. As he did so, one of the rival gang members threw a bayonet towards him, narrowly missing him. Before running off, the thrower shouted, 'There's your body over there.' Brady found his brother, covered in blood oozing from the many wounds about his face and on his body. Young Brady spoke to his brother but got no answer. John Brady was dead.

Police were called, as was an ambulance, and a full-scale murder investigation was soon in place. All known members of the 'Dougie Boys' gang were rounded up that night and quizzed well into the early hours of the next morning. Statements were obtained during door-to-door inquiries from the many witnesses who had been looking or hanging out of their windows of their tenement houses, watching the running battle unfold below them. Very soon, police had a reasonably complete picture of what had taken place in various streets, and more importantly, who had been responsible.

A postmortem examination was carried out on Brady's body early the following morning. It was discovered that Brady had died from a stab wound to the chest which had sliced through a corner of his heart and continued on to puncture a lung. His blood, escaping from the heart, filled his lungs and he had drowned in his own blood. A total of 16 knife wounds were counted on Brady's body. Most had been inflicted by what the pathologist termed was 'a long knife'. When asked by police if that could mean a bayonet-type weapon, the medical opinion was that it was most likely.

On the Sunday evening, less than 24 hours after the murder of John Brady, police swooped on a number of homes in the Govanhill area of the city. At one, the home of brothers Hugh, Robert and Alexander Crosbie at 150 Jamieson Street, the detectives made four arrests – the aforementioned Crosbies and their brother-in-law John Lyons, who also resided there. At another Govanhill address, Patrick Joseph Houston, was also arrested after his home had been thoroughly searched. After being interviewed, all five men were charged with the murder of John Brady and appeared at the Marine Police Court, where they were remanded for further inquiry. They were later detained in Barlinnie Prison, during which time, Robert Crosbie (25) and Patrick Houston (27), were released after their alibis were checked and verified.

However, the police made a further arrest when, acting on information supplied to them, they visited another house, this time in the Paisley area and detained 25-year-old John Alexander Lennie. He was a war veteran who had spent five years in the army after being called up from the Territorials. Only recently had he been invalided out of the forces due to injury. Eight weeks after their arrests, at Glasgow High Court, in the North Court, Lord MacKay sat in judgement as a jury of nine men and six women were empanelled. This was the first case in Glasgow to revert to a full-strength jury after the war years when a jury usually only consisted of seven members.

Four men stood in the dock accused of murder and other charges; they were 21-year-old John Lyon, 25-year-old John Alexander Lennie and brothers Hugh Crosbie and Alexander Crosbie, 28 and 17 years old respectively. All four pled not guilty to all the charges and each lodged a special defence of alibi in relation to the charges. As was usual, witnesses came and went at regular intervals as the evidence mounted. A large proportion of the evidence centred on the identification of the persons accused of being involved in the fracas.

A tram driver and conductress identified all of the accused as getting on and off their tramcar in Argyle Street and of their general behaviour. Other witnesses identified one, two or more of the accused as being involved in the disorder. Most damning of all was when Joseph Brady identified John Lyon as the person who threw the bayonet at him as Lyon walked away from his brother's body.

One witness who gave surprising evidence was the aforementioned John McFarlane who admitted to being a member of the 'Dougie Boys' and of being involved on 20th October. His evidence was that he had also attended an identification parade at a police office on the evening of 17th November, during which he picked out two or three people on the parade and identified them as being present and being part of the disorder. His evidence changed somewhat in the courtroom.

McFarlane stated to the court that he had picked out the youths 'because he had seen them before'. He further added that he did not see anyone at the identification parade that he had seen that night in Washington Street. He explained that he had only seen the backs of men in Washington Street and when the four accused were asked to stand in the dock with their backs to the witness box, McFarlane said, 'I still cannot identify them.' An angry exchange then followed between McFarlane and the Advocate-Depute, Mr Sinclair Shaw KC, who commented, 'I suggest that since the parade you have changed your mind?' McFarlane replied indignantly, 'I am under oath now. I was not under oath then.'

Another witness and self-confessed 'Dougie Boy', 17-year-old Thomas Montgomery of Hinshaw Street, Maryhill, positively identified both Lennie and Alexander Crosbie as being part of the group who were chasing Joseph Smyth in Brown Street. Montgomery did add that he did not see Lennie holding any weapons. Thomas Fenton, a resident of Washington Street, told the court of the gang fighting in his street and of how John Brady ended up on his back, his head resting in the gutter of the roadway with his face streaked red with blood.

After a full day of prosecution evidence, it was now the turn of the defence to present their case. Their evidence centred on testimony supporting their special defence of alibi. Three of the accused, the two Crosbies and Lyon gave evidence on their own behalf. During their time in the witness box, each denied being a member of any gang. Their alibi was that they were in and out of each other's company on the night of 20th October and all were in the Govanhill area. At one point during the evening, all were together, along with others, on the corner of Cathcart Road and Aikenhead Road for over an hour, allegedly discussing dog racing. This was between 9.15 and 10.15pm.

Later, about 11pm, while Alexander Crosbie was in his home in Jamieson Street, he was asked to go to a local chip shop to buy chips for supper. He refused so Mrs Hugh Crosbie and Mrs John Lyons went instead. Whilst in the shop, they were joined by their husbands, and all four went home from there. No one left the family home after this time. A number of independent witnesses were called to corroborate various parts of the alibi and did so with the minimum of fuss or contradiction.

Lennie's alibi was slightly different. He did admit to being on a tramcar in Argyle Street on the night of the murder. He also admitted that he had got on the tram at the Central Station bridge with a large group of young males whose behaviour was disorderly. However, he did not get off with them as they alighted at Washington Street. Lennie's alibi was that he remained on the tramcar until getting off at Finnieston Street. He therefore could not have taken part in any disturbances.

The trial lasted five days and the jury was sent out on Saturday morning to consider their verdict. They returned an hour later. They had unanimously found John Lyon, John Alexander Lennie and Alexander Crosbie guilty of all charges. The charge of murder against Hugh Crosbie was found 'not proven' by a majority. However, he was unanimously found guilty of the other two charges, assault and breach of the peace. Lord MacKay pointed out the seriousness of the crimes and the fact that he had two previous convictions for similar offences. He sentenced him to three years' penal servitude on these charges.

In relation to the other three accused, Lord MacKay donned the black cap as he sentenced Lyon, Lennie and Crosbie to death, the execution to take place at Barlinnie Prison on 5th January 1946. The guilty showed no trace of emotion and all four turned in the dock and made their way down the stairs to the cells below. A loud round of applause sprang up from the public benches. As the accused disappeared from sight, one of them shouted,

'Happy New Year.' Almost before the cell doors had closed, intimation was being made of the intention to appeal. One of the most compelling arguments was that Alexander Crosbie was only 17 years of age and the law quite clearly stated that no one under the age of 18 could be sentenced to death. The reality was that Crosbie had been born on 15th December 1927 at 10.10pm. Eighteen years later, on 15th December 1945, he had been sentenced to death almost ten hours before his 'birthday'. Appeals for all four convicted prisoners were duly lodged and all of them cited misdirection of the jury by the judge, Lord MacKay, and also that the verdict was inconsistent, unreasonable and contradictory considering the evidence heard during the trial. As is the case, the executions were suspended pending the outcome of the appeals.

In the middle of January 1946, the Court of Criminal Appeal in Edinburgh heard the appeal. Legal submissions were made and the testimony of a new witness was also heard by the four appeal judges. After three and a half days of argument, on Monday 21st January, the judges unanimously dismissed the appeals of all four prisoners. A new date of 8th February was fixed for the executions. In the interim period, petitions were raised to have the death penalties on Lennie, Lyon and Alexander Crosbie rescinded. Within days, thousands of people from all over Scotland had signed the petitions, which were then forwarded to the Secretary of State for Scotland.

Late on Tuesday night, 5th February, the Lord Provost of Glasgow received notification from the Scottish Office that the death sentences on both Alexander Crosbie and John Lennie had been commuted and would be replaced with a sentence of penal servitude for life. When the Lord Provost and his deputy called at Barlinnie to inform the prisoners of this decision, neither showed any trace of emotion. The effort to reprieve John Lyon continued. It was to no avail. The authorities stated that there were no grounds for a reprieve and at two minutes past eight o'clock on the morning of Friday 8th February 1946, John Lyon took his last steps at Barlinnie Prison, Glasgow.

Police officers on duty outside the prison gates, in the semi-darkness of the cold morning, kept between 60 and 70 supporters and spectators away from the grounds of the jail. The first indication that the sentence had been completed came just after 8.13am when a short typewritten note was pinned to the outside of the gates. It simply stated that the sentence had been carried out. Lyon's body was than buried within the confines of the prison grounds. The crowd slowly dispersed. Lyon's execution was Barlinnie Prison's first ever execution. It was also the first execution in Glasgow since August 1928, when George Reynolds was executed at Duke Street Prison for the murder of a bakehouse foreman.

Glasgow Police set up a special task force to try and break up the gangs and took to patrolling the streets in radio-controlled cars and vans in an effort to respond to gang fights and disturbances quicker than usual. Courts were asked to impose harsh sentences on those who were caught, which they did. No matter what was tried, the gangs flourished.

The fight to control the spectre of gangs, and their ever incumbent violence, continues to this day …

Chapter 18

Eglinton Street, October 1948

As stated in the introduction, almost all of the crimes featured in this book have been replicated to some degree. The case presented in this chapter is one of the exceptions. William Park was a 42-year-old married man who resided with his wife, Mary, and their five children in a two-bedroomed apartment at 487 Eglinton Street on Glasgow's south side. William earned a decent wage in his employment as a railwayman, working in the local railway yards at Salkeld Street and Kilbirnie Street. His wife was a full-time housewife. By all accounts, the Park family were very well thought of by their friends and neighbours. They were well respected in the neighbourhood and are said to have doted on their five children, Dorothy (15), Mary (14), Margaret (13) Wilma (12), and the youngest Duncan, who was aged eight.

So what was the catalyst that caused William Park and his wife Mary, or both, to try and kill themselves and their five children one evening in October 1948? On Tuesday 5th October that year, Glaswegians woke up to the headline 'Seven Found Gassed' in the morning newspaper. Reading behind the headlines, a stunned and shocked public discovered that a neighbour at 487 Eglinton Street had smelled gas during the night or early morning and had called on police to investigate. When two police officers arrived at the close mouth, they managed to trace the source of the escaping gas to the ground floor flat belonging to the Park's.

Despite repeated hammering on the door by the officers, they could get no answer. When the police eventually broke it open they found that the kitchen was filled with gas fumes and all seven members of the family were lying in various places around the room. All of them were unconscious. Medical assistance was sent for but by the time it arrived, the oldest girl, Dorothy, was dead. A number of ambulances then arrived at the scene and the remaining members of the family were removed to the Victoria Infirmary without delay. All six were admitted in a state of coma induced by coal gas inhalation.

Back at the house, the two police constables who had first attended the scene, called in their detective colleagues. They found that all the kitchen windows, doors and chimney vents had been sealed off using sticky tape and newspaper and the gas jets in the room had been switched full on but not lit. They decided that they were dealing with a case of murder and detectives were stationed at the bedsides of both parents, awaiting them regaining consciousness. During this period, a second child, 14-year-old Mary, died the day following the grim discovery. She had never regained consciousness. On Wednesday afternoon, 6th October, a third child, 13-year-old Margaret, also passed away, again without ever coming to. It wasn't until much later that day that the other two younger children and both parents began to show signs of recovery by emerging from their comas.

Thursday and Friday of that week was spent slowly recouping their strength and William and Mary Park were interviewed separately, but tentatively, by waiting detectives. Neither would admit to any form of wrongdoing. Instead, they claimed no knowledge of events. By Saturday morning, all surviving members of the family were considered fit enough to be discharged from hospital but with their home being classed as a murder scene, the family had nowhere to go. That problem was resolved when, in the afternoon, the two remaining children – Wilma and Duncan – were taken into the care of Glasgow Corporation Welfare Services, while detectives arrested their parents and charged them with three counts of murder and two of attempted murder. Both appeared on Monday morning in the local district court where the charges were again put to them. Neither made any plea or declaration and they were remanded in custody pending further inquiry. During their detention in prison, the Park's met up once at the funeral of their three daughters, who were buried together. They attended the service in the company of their respective prison warders and were returned to jail immediately upon the completion of the interment.

The Park's trial began at Glasgow High Court on Thursday 7th December 1948, and it caught the public's attention. Both husband and wife pled not guilty to murdering three of their children and the attempted murder of the other two. Both parents lodged defences of 'mental weakness' in answer to the accusations. Yet again at a major murder trial in Glasgow, not one free seat could be found in the court. Outside, crowds milled around the court building, eager for any snippet of news from inside the courtroom.

First up was evidence for the prosecution. The police officers involved explained how the kitchen area, and only that room, had been totally sealed off from the rest of the house and the outside world. Even the keyhole in the kitchen door had a piece of tape placed over it. Medical evidence was also to the fore, indicating that all three deaths were as a result of asphyxiation due to coal gas inhalation. By lunchtime, the prosecution case had been completed and it was the turn of the defence. First to give his account of the sorry tale was William Park. He told a hushed court that on the Friday evening prior to the event, he and his wife had discovered that their eldest daughter, 15-year-old Dorothy, was pregnant. What followed for the rest of that night was a family discussion involving him, his wife and his daughter.

Park freely admitted that a number of matters had deeply disturbed him. One of them was that Dorothy had refused to reveal the identity of the expectant father. Another important fact was that Dorothy was more than five months pregnant and therefore, beyond any possible consideration for an illegal abortion. Park further stated that his wife had basically offered nothing to the family discussion other than to cry continuously and whine about the disgrace that was being brought upon the family. She was of no use in trying to find a solution to the problems now confronting them. For the remainder of the weekend, she appeared to be 'in a trance' and would not, or could not, sleep. She also continually took large doses of aspirin at regular intervals. Eventually, on Sunday night, Mrs Park collapsed through exhaustion and her husband managed to revive her and put her to bed. He did, at one point, take her a cup of tea to aid her recovery. However, when cross-examined on this part of his evidence, he could give no satisfactory answer as to why his wife was found slumped in the kitchen with the rest of the family. Instead, he claimed he could remember nothing after five pm on the Sunday evening.

Park was further pressed by the Advocate Depute, Mr Leechman. He denied a suggestion that he had entered into a pact with his wife to murder the children and then 'do away with themselves'. At one stage in his evidence, Park declared that he, and he alone, 'might' have decided to do away with the family and he was almost certain that this is what happened. He quickly added, adamantly, that if he had been sane, it would not have occurred. Even so, he could not tell the court how it had all taken place as he had no recollection of events, which to him suggested that he was not guilty. Park was stating to the court that while he could have been the person who taped up all windows, doors and chimney outlets and turned on the gas jets, because of his mental condition, or 'mental weakness', at this time, he was not guilty of murder.

Mrs Park then gave evidence to the court and she informed them that she was greatly upset to discover her eldest child's pregnancy. She told of hearing remarks from neighbours about how her daughter was becoming quite stout and 'putting on weight'. As a consequence, she had taken Dorothy to their doctor on Friday afternoon and he soon discovered the true reason for her increased girth. Mrs Park admitted that she did not get any sleep for two days after the revelations and she eventually collapsed. Her next recollection is of waking up in hospital and of being told that her children had been gassed and that three had died. She insisted that she loved all of her children and could never, ever, think of any occasion where she might want to harm them.

When Mrs Park finished giving her evidence, the defence case ended. The trial was adjourned for the day, only to resume the following morning. Speeches by both crown and defence counsel along with the summing up by Lord Jamieson took up most of the next morning's business before the jury were asked to retire to consider their verdict. It took them only 25 minutes to deliberate before returning to the courtroom. By a unanimous verdict, they found both Mr and Mrs Park guilty as charged. Pandemonium swept through the court. It took police fully three or four minutes to restore order to the courtroom. When it finally calmed down, there were quite a number of spaces to be seen in the previously crammed public benches. Those who had left had done so in order to be amongst the first to pass on the news of the convictions to others. There was no need to wait to find out what the Park's punishment was going to be. There could only be one sentence passed on them – death.

Lord Jamieson told the couple, 'You have, after a fair trial, been found guilty by a jury of your fellow citizens. You have been found guilty of murder and there is only one sentence and one sentence alone which I can pronounce.' The black cap was placed on his head when he uttered the final words, ' … which is pronounced for doom.' The execution was set for 29th December at Barlinnie Prison for William Park and the Prison of Glasgow in Duke Street for Mrs Park. As both prisoners were being led from the dock down the stairs to the cells below, Mrs Park was seen by many onlookers to stumble or faint and was observed being held upright by her husband and a policewoman.

Almost immediately, appeals were lodged with the Scottish Court of Criminal Appeal; the grounds being that the trial judge had misdirected the jury on a number of points. The four main points being that he had told the jury that if the Parks knew what they were doing then a verdict of culpable homicide should not be considered; that unless the intention to kill was negated, then the crime was murder; that the jury were misled on the defence of 'mental weakness' and on the evidence required to substantiate it; and lastly that the judge, by the content in his summing up, left the jury with no alternative to the murder verdict.

In the appeal case for Mrs Park, further grounds were raised in that Lord Jamieson misdirected the jury by referring to defence evidence as showing that Mr and Mrs Park had agreed to commit the crimes with which they were charged, when in fact, the evidence led pointed to Mrs Park being free from any blame. The defence teams also petitioned the Court of Appeal for a re-opening of the trial in order to hear evidence from two doctors regarding evidence of the Park's 'diminished responsibility'.

From court papers, it would appear that the defence had, at the time of the trial, statements from the two doctors about Mr and Mrs Park's mental state, but it was decided not to call the doctors as witnesses. However, after their conviction and sentence, one of the doctors contacted the defence team and stated that he now wished to amend his original statement. When contacted with the 'new' information, the other doctor involved, concurred with his colleague's 'new' opinion.

The appeal hearing lasted for over four hours. At the end of it all, the Court of Appeal dismissed the application. It was decreed that the trial judge had acted correctly in summing up the evidence for the jury. It was also decided that the re-opening of a High Court trial to hear 'new' evidence was not an option that the Scottish law lords were prepared to sanction. A new date for the execution was fixed for 14th January 1949.

Almost immediately, a petition was started for the reprieve of the Parks. It was begun by the Hutchestown and Gorbals Municipal wards and Mrs Alice Cullen, Labour MP for Gorbals. Within five days, over 22,000 people signed the petition. However, before it could be presented to the authorities, on 6th January 1949, a letter was received from the Scottish Office stating that the Secretary of State for Scotland 'had felt justified in advising the King to commute the capital sentence against both accused ... '. They would undertake penal servitude for life instead.

Yet, less than four years later, both were released from their life sentences and they quietly disappeared from Glasgow. The news about their release became public in early December 1952, six weeks after their liberation. When asked, the Scottish Office refused to discuss the matter in detail and would only state ' ... long term prisoners' cases are reviewed at regular intervals by the Secretary of State'. Attempts to find out the reasons behind the early release of the Parks have been met with silence ever since. The standard reply is simply that records of this type are sealed for at least 75 years.

No track was kept of the surviving children Wilma and Duncan Park and as a consequence, nothing is known of what became of them.

Chapter 19
Prospecthill Road, July 1950

Sixty-two-year-old taxi driver John Kennedy was in a good mood. He had just dropped off a hire in Kilmarnock and the cost of the fare meant that he could take the rest of the night off – and it wasn't even one am yet! When Kennedy drove along Prospecthill Road on Glasgow's south side early that Friday morning of 28th July 1950 on his way to his Rutherglen home, he had no idea what was about to happen to him.

As he approached the junction of Aikenhead Road, the headlights of his cab picked out what he thought at first to be a bundle of old clothes lying in the roadway. As soon as Kennedy stopped his vehicle, he quickly realised that his first impressions were wrong. The bundle of clothes turned out to be the severely twisted and mangled body of a woman. In a state of shock, Kennedy went to the public phone box just across the road and called for the police. He returned to his vehicle and sat patiently waiting for the police to arrive, the lights of his car illuminating the scene. As he stared at the horror in front of him, the crew of a passing Glasgow Corporation cleansing lorry stopped to speak to him. The driver, Samuel Murray, and his mate David Ashe, told Kennedy they had passed that particular spot ten minutes ago and had seen a black car sitting there but there was no body on the road. Together, all three men waited for the police to arrive. When the police appeared on the scene, they immediately cordoned off the entire area. They suspected it to be a hit-and-run road accident. Statements were taken from the three witnesses at the scene and as is usual in fatal road accidents, the specialist Traffic Department were called for.

Traffic officer, 45-year-old PC William Kevan arrived, and the first thing he noticed was that the woman's body was lying on top of two distinct sets of skid marks. However, even to the uninformed eye, there was something strange about these marks. One set were straight while the other set were curved. Closer examination revealed that the skid marks were made by a car (or cars) going in opposite directions. There was also a number of other facts that just didn't add up for the experienced constable. The victim's shoes were lying on the roadway, some distance from the body, as was her handbag.

They were separated by a distance of over 40 yards from the body.

As far as PC Kevan could tell, there appeared to be no injuries to the lower legs of the victim, nor was there any trace of vehicle debris – headlamp glass or mud from a vehicle's underside. From all this evidence, the constable could reach only one conclusion – the victim had not been standing upright when she was struck by the mystery vehicle. Kevan called in the CID.

The traffic officer's initial suspicions were verified before the morning was much older. A police casualty surgeon, called to the scene, was able to confirm a lack of injuries to the dead woman's legs, and when this was added to all the other evidence from the locus, it led to one conclusion – this was a case of murder. As is usual when the victim of a crime is unidentified, the newspapers of the day were asked for their assistance. However, they were informed that the female was the victim of a hit-and-run road accident. Nonetheless, some experienced reporters could smell a different story, probably because they were well aware that the CID never involved themselves in traffic cases. No matter, the publicity had the desired effect. Within hours of the first editions reaching the news-stands, the victim was identified.

A woman from Nicholson Street in the Gorbals area of Glasgow contacted the police. The previous night she had been asked by a neighbour, 40-year-old Catherine McClusky, if she could babysit her child. McClusky had said that she had some very important matters to take care of. When she still hadn't returned to pick up her three-month-old baby by the next morning, the neighbour had become quite anxious. A description provided by the neighbour was identical to that of the victim. Very quickly, teams of detectives moved into Nicholson Street and began door-to-door enquiries. It didn't take too long before the police had what they call, 'a definite line of enquiry to follow'. Catherine McClusky's neighbours told police how she regularly boasted that the father of her youngest child was a policeman and that he had to pay her weekly maintenance.

McClusky's older sister, Elizabeth Coggans, was interviewed and stated that one day recently, she had accompanied her sister to the local Welfare Office and on their return, had met with a uniformed police officer who was on patrol. Her sister spent almost 15 minutes talking to him, during which time, Coggans alleged that she could hear the occasional angry word being exchanged. McClusky later confided in her that the policeman was the father of her young child. The final piece of the jigsaw fell into place when at least two of the victim's friends mentioned that the policeman lover drove a large black car. The trail led detectives to Glasgow police constable D.138, James

Robertson. He was known to have a large black Austin motorcar, which he had explained to his colleagues at Gorbals Police Station, belonged to a relative of his and he was looking after it.

As Robertson was on night shift that week, the detectives decided to question his beat colleague, Constable David Moffat, first. He was able to state that on the night in question, he and Robertson left the police office and they both got into Robertson's car. Together, they went to their beat, which was in the area of Cumberland Street. They hadn't been walking on the beat long when Robertson declared that he had to leave. He explained that he was 'going to take a blonde home'. Moffat never saw Robertson again until just after one am the next morning, and when he did, he couldn't help but notice that Robertson was sweating profusely and his shirt collar was soaking wet. Robertson explained his condition away as being due to his car having broken its exhaust pipe and he had made attempts to repair it.

All this information was enough for Robertson to be brought in for questioning. His home at 51 Craigmuir Street, Glasgow, which he shared with his wife and two children, was searched and 14 car registration books and a car radio were recovered. When Robertson's locker was searched at the police office, a rubber cosh was found in his uniform raincoat pocket. When questioned, Robertson told detectives where to find the black Austin motorcar – in a lockup garage in Gorbals Street. When it was located, it was forensically examined. Traces of blood and hair were found on the car's chassis. When the licence plate DYS 570 was checked out later, it was found to belong to a tractor owned by a farmer from Aberdeenshire.

Robertson was charged with Catherine McClusky's murder and appeared in court the day after his arrest. After being remanded in custody, he was told to put on his police uniform for the last time and to take his place in an identity parade. Every other participant in the line-up was a serving uniformed police officer. The parade was then viewed by relatives and friends of the murdered woman. Each person who viewed the line-up selected Robertson as the man they had seen associating with Catherine McClusky.

As Robertson languished in Barlinnie Prison, the case against him was being built up by detectives. By the time the trial opened, in the infamous North Court of Glasgow's High Court building on November 6th 1950, the list of witnesses cited for the case was the longest in living memory. The case also attracted the public's curiosity and brought out the crowds. Seats were at a premium as the queues of hopeful spectators snaked around the block from early morning. Robertson went on trial facing three charges. He was accused of murdering Catherine McClusky by striking her on the head with a rubber truncheon or other similar instrument or alternatively rendering her unconscious by other means and thereafter driving a vehicle over her. He was also charged with stealing the motor car from a city centre street in May 1950, while the third, and last charge, accused Robertson of breaking into a car showroom and stealing 14 log books and a car radio, during the month of April. Most of the evidence presented to the court by the prosecution was technical in relation to the motor vehicle and forensic with regard to the victim's injuries.

At one stage in the proceedings, a most unusual occurrence took place when the jury were taken from the courtroom, along with the judge, into the back yard of the court building adjoining Mart Street. Once there, they found themselves looking at the black Austin motorcar, DYS 570. The vehicle had been lifted onto its side so that the jury could have an uninterrupted and close-up view of the entire underside of the car. This was especially important in relation to evidence the jury were to hear later during the trial.

Both doctors Andrew Allison and James Imrie, the latter being Glasgow Police Chief Medical Officer, gave the jury graphic descriptions of the events, as they saw it, and of the injuries suffered by McClusky. Her jaw was broken in three separate places. There were fractures to her nose, breast bone, pelvis and numerous ribs. Most of her left ear was torn completely away. Altogether, the doctors listed over 30 external injuries and several internal ones, and it came as no surprise to anyone in the courtroom when they gave their opinion that death was due to multiple injuries. Dr Allison stated that the injuries on McClusky had been 'more gross than he had ever met in an accident with a private car'.

The doctors were both adamant and positive that the victim was lying on the roadway when first struck by the motor car. Somewhat chillingly, they added that they were also sure that McClusky was not dead at this point in time. Both medical men were of the opinion that McClusky had received a blow to the head which had merely stunned her, possibly rendering her unconscious, and that her fatal injuries came from the motor vehicle.

A procession of witnesses was called to tell of the life of Catherine McClusky. Most were neighbours from the tenements of Nicholson Street, as in that type of dwelling, very few secrets, if any, could be kept. Everyone knew everyone else's business.

McClusky was a single woman who had two children, both boys. One was six years of age while the other had only been born in April of that year. A woman officer from the Department of Welfare testified that McClusky had refused on a number of occasions to reveal the identity of the father of her youngest child and as a result, her weekly benefits were cut accordingly. Perhaps this was the reason for the argument in the car that fateful night. McClusky's income had been drastically reduced and she had another mouth to feed and body to clothe. She was obviously looking to Robertson to make up the difference. He couldn't or wouldn't do it.

Perhaps he thought that a further eight shillings leaving his already meagre weekly paypacket would be noticed by his wife. This was certainly the route taken by the prosecution. It suggested that the motive for murder was because Robertson was being blackmailed by McClusky and could no longer take it.

Surprisingly, Robertson gave evidence on his own behalf. He stood in the witness box, slightly stooped but tall and thin. His hands were clasped loosely behind his back. He stated that he had met Catherine McClusky the previous year in the course of his duties when he had been called to her home to deal with a disturbance. He had met her a few times since that date.

When asked by his counsel if he was the father of her new baby, Robertson denied the matter. He had met her a few times and they were on friendly terms. So much so, McClusky asked to meet him that fateful Thursday night and Robertson duly obliged, slipping away from his beat.

The situation regarding the stolen vehicle was then dealt with. Robertson admitted lying to his colleagues at work in saying that he was looking after it for a relative. He did admit that he had 'noticed' the car lying on some spare ground one morning and had 'kept an eye on it' for a few days. When he decided it was abandoned, he obtained a key for it and began using it and fitted false plates to it. In relation to the charge of the theft of the 14 car registration books and other items, Robertson merely said that he had found these in a backcourt when he was patrolling his beat and had kept them out of curiosity.

Robertson's evidence continued on to state that he and McClusky argued in the car about her wanting to be taken to the village of Neilston in Renfrewshire. Robertson thought that this would take too long (it was at least eight miles away) and would add to the time he had already spent being absent from his beat. By this time, Robertson was driving in Prospecthill Road. McClusky became hysterical and demanded to be allowed out of the vehicle. Robertson stopped the car and after McClusky got out, he drove off. According to Robertson, he had driven no more than 100 yards when he had a sudden change of heart and decided that he could not leave McClusky all alone and far from home at that time in the morning.

He reversed the vehicle, not particularly fast, but when he heard a dull thud, he stopped the car and got out to investigate. He was horrified to see the bloodied face of Catherine McClusky staring up at him from under the running board of the vehicle. He decided very quickly that from her condition, she was obviously dead.

By the light of his torch, Robertson could see that the body of McClusky was trapped under the car. According to him, her dress and coat were entangled with the prop shaft. He tried many times to free her body but without success. He then came up with the idea of driving the vehicle back and forward several times until the body freed itself. Robertson claimed that he had waited around the scene, wondering what to do next, but then he drove off when he saw the headlights of another car approaching in Prospecthill Road.

It is strange that Robertson gave this reason as an excuse in his evidence. He had been present earlier in the trial when the jury had viewed the Austin car in the yard of the court building. He had obviously heard the evidence when it was offered that this particular model of car had a completely enclosed prop shaft, therefore making it impossible for anything to become trapped in its workings. It might have been more feasible, and believable, bearing in mind his excuses to Constable Moffat, to suggest that McClusky's body had become caught up in the vehicle exhaust pipe.

Robertson parked the vehicle near to his beat and resumed his patrol, meeting up with Constable Moffat. One of the first things Robertson did was to pen an entry in the beat journal of the Cumberland Street police signal box. It read: 'At 12.50am today, a woman was knocked down and fatally injured in Prospecthill Road near Aitkenhead Road. The motor car, believed to be a small blue Austin, maybe 10hp was driven by a man wearing a light fawn Burberry coat. The car did not stop and was last seen driving citywards on Aitkenhead Road.'

Having given his version of events, Robertson was then cross-examined by Mr Leslie, the Advocate Depute. It was during this period of questioning that Robertson amazingly stated, 'I was never very friendly with her'. Mr Leslie put it to the prisoner that when McClusky became hysterical in the car, he produced his rubber cosh from his uniform raincoat and hit her on the head, knocking her unconscious. He then pushed her out of the car and then ran over her a number of times. Robertson, of course, denied it all.

Robertson continued to defend himself in the witness box. He admitted that while he was undoubtedly a thief and a liar, he was not a murderer. He maintained that what had happened to Catherine McClusky had been an unfortunate accident – nothing more. Robertson's evidence lasted just under two hours and the remainder of the defence case involved the evidence of expert witnesses to try and confirm the 'accident' scenario. By the end of the defence evidence, it was late on Friday afternoon. The trial had lasted an unexpected five days. The jury of eight men and seven women were taken from the court and ensconced in a city centre hotel for the weekend and guarded by police.

On the resumption of proceedings on Monday, the jury listened to the finishing arguments of both prosecution and defence, which took up most of the day. It was almost five pm when they left the court to consider their verdict. It took them an hour before they returned. Robertson stood with his head bowed as the verdict was delivered. The jury unanimously found him guilty of both theft charges and guilty, by a majority, of the murder of Catherine McClusky. He showed no emotion whatsoever as the judge, Lord Keith, informed him that there was no other sentence he could deliver other than the death penalty. Almost on the judge's last word, Robertson turned away and hurried down the stairs from the dock to the cells below and out of sight.

Even though it was late evening, large crowds had gathered around the High Court building. Police had to force a way through the crowd to allow the prison van to leave the yard with Robertson on board, bound for Barlinnie Prison. Most of the spectators shouted, cheered, applauded, while some banged on the side of the van as it passed.

As usual, an appeal against the sentence was raised but quickly dismissed by the authorities. Confidential information suggests that Robertson remained in high spirits, never for one minute thinking he would suffer the ultimate penalty. As his judgement day grew ever closer, the same sources state that Robertson became more reclusive and withdrawn as the finality of his situation slowly sunk in.

Early in the morning of Friday 16th December 1950, James Ronald Robertson, or 'Big Ronnie' as he was known to most people, was hanged at Barlinnie Prison, Glasgow. His body was placed in a simple coffin and buried within the prison walls.

Legal opinion suggests that Robertson could have saved himself from the gallows, if only he had admitted to his affair with Catherine McClusky. However, he refused to do so, probably to save his wife and children from further embarrassment.

Chapter 20
Hyndland Road, August 1952

In 1952, Edwin Finlay was 18 years old. He came from a good family, and had been privately educated at Glasgow High School. Finlay appeared to be set for a lucrative career in the world of banking and finance. He was employed as a bank clerk and was in the third year of his apprenticeship with the British Linen Bank, working at the Kelvinhaugh branch at 1190 Argyle Street. In his spare time, Finlay was a regular churchgoer and a Sunday schoolteacher. He still met up with and socialised with his ex-school friends and was considered, by all who knew him, to be a quiet, shy and very reserved individual. So what turned this young man into a baby-faced killer?

No one can say for sure when Finlay actually 'lost the plot' but the evidence, as we shall see, was there for all to see. On Friday 29th August, when the bank closed, Edwin's pockets bulged more than usual but nobody noticed. When Finlay failed to turn up on Saturday morning to open the bank, nobody was too concerned but after substitute keys were found, staff discovered that money was missing from the branch's emergency fund. And it wasn't just £5 or £10 – it was £1220, the value mainly made up of US dollars.

Police at Partick Police Station were notified and immediately began an investigation into the matter. Officers were despatched to Finlay's home at 65 Marlborough Avenue in Broomhill, but his mother and father had no idea where their son was. He had left that morning to go to work as usual. Police also interviewed friends of Finlay. They all told a similar story that Edwin had been flashing a wad of bank notes around in a local café and claiming that he 'had robbed the bank'. Edwin wasn't known as a person who joked or bragged about such things but on this occasion every one of his friends thought that he was playing a prank on them.

As the police looked for him that Saturday, Finlay was sitting in the departure lounge of Renfrew Airport, waiting to board a flight to Dublin. On his arrival in the Irish capital Finlay booked himself into one of the city's top hotels, using his own name. He passed himself off as an army officer, home on leave from the war in Korea. Finlay then visited a gunsmith shop in the city and spun them the same lie that he was a British army officer on leave. He further intimated to the shop assistant, that like many of his brother officers, he found the army issue .45 revolvers far too heavy a weapon to wield with any accuracy in the heat of battle. He was looking to purchase something lighter in weight and with more accuracy. After being shown various weapons, Finlay decided to purchase an Italian-made automatic pistol, a .22 Beretta. He also purchased a large quantity of ammunition for the weapon.

What happened next is the first anomaly in the case. Under Irish law, Finlay could not legally purchase the weapon without first having a firearms certificate issued by the local authorities. This he did not have nor did he stand any chance of getting one, because he was a visitor to the country. But for some unknown reason, the shop assistant handed over the weapon and ammunition without any question. Finlay paid for the weapon and walked out of the shop with it in his pocket. He spent the remainder of his break in the Irish capital sightseeing.

One extravagance was the purchase, or intended purchase, of a motor-cycle from a company located in Baggot Street. Unfortunately, when he tried out the motorcycle on a test run, he crashed and injured his leg, which gave him a limp for a number of days. Not put off by this mishap, Finlay left a deposit on the machine and the instruction that when he returned to Scotland, he would forward the remainder of the purchase price and the motorcycle was to be shipped to him then. Another story goes that Finlay bought two more pistols while in Dublin but this is untrue. While Finlay had purchased two firearms, a .38 Webley revolver and a .22 Spanish automatic pistol, he had bought them from a firm of Glasgow auctioneers. These weapons had been innocently, but wrongly, classified as antiques and could be obtained without a firearms' certificate.

On Thursday afternoon, 4th September, Finlay flew back from Dublin into Renfrew Airport – and a place in Scottish criminal history. One of the first things he did on his return was to telephone his 'girlfriend', 17-year-old Ann Frier, who lived in Whittinghame Drive in the West End, just off Great Western Road. She was not at home, but her mother spoke with Finlay. After their conversation finished, Mrs Frier contacted Finlay's parents and informed them that he had been in touch. They, in turn, notified the police of their runaway son's reappearance. Finlay, it is believed, thought of Ann Frier as his girlfriend but due to his shyness and introverted behaviour, he failed to communicate any of his feelings to her. So he worshipped her from a distance but convinced himself that she was his girlfriend.

The officers engaged in investigating the theft of money from the bank decided it might be worthwhile sending out a couple of officers to the area of the Western Tennis Club on Hyndland Road in the West End. Ann Frier was a member of the club and usually played there on Thursday evenings. The police were aware that Finlay knew about this and considered it a possibility that he might try to intercept the young girl at the club premises. Two constables, 31-year-old John Macleod and 29-year-old Thomas MacDonald, both in plain clothes, were instructed to go to Hyndland Road, keeping a lookout for Finlay and if they spotted him, bring him in for questioning about the missing money. Both officers thought of it as nothing more than a normal everyday job. How hard could it be to detain a spotty-faced lad of 18 years?

Finlay went from the airport to Glasgow city centre, where he booked into the St Enoch Hotel. He then called at the left luggage department of the railway station next to the hotel. He produced a ticket and redeemed a leather briefcase which contained the two 'antique' firearms. Finlay removed the pistols, stuffing them into the pockets of his coat. He then took a large quantity of bank notes and placed them in the briefcase, which he duly returned to the left luggage attendant for safekeeping. After this, Finlay visited a café in Crow Road where he met up with some of his friends, but Finlay was not his usual quiet self. He attracted attention to himself by behaving like the life and soul of the group. He flashed wads of cash, buying coffees, ice cream and drinks for all and once again joked that he 'had robbed the bank'. But his friends weren't laughing; they knew he had robbed the bank; most of them had been interviewed by police in the days before, trying to shed some light on Finlay's whereabouts. At one quiet moment, Finlay produced one of his guns and showed it to one of his friends who was duly impressed as Finlay twirled the pistol on his forefinger before thrusting it back into the pocket of his gabardine coat.

Soon enough, Finlay left the café and made his way to Hyndland Road. He walked up and down the road outside the tennis club, occasionally peering in to see if he could see Ann Frier. They had met at Sunday school in Balshagray Church, where Finlay had been the teacher and she a member. They had been out on one 'date', where they walked and talked for about two hours. Finlay had also sent her a Valentine's card. She had seen him occasionally since then and had spoken to him once or twice but hadn't seen him for about seven weeks prior to the theft. She had been told earlier in the week by police that he was missing from home and she thought it may have had something to do with Finlay having been called up for National Service which he was due to start at the end of September.

Hyndland Road, August 1952

Just before eight pm, Constables Macleod and MacDonald spotted Finlay walking away from the tennis club and along Hyndland Road towards the junction with Great Western Road. Both officers crossed over the road and came up behind Finlay. Macleod was closest to the youth and it was he who spoke first. He said, 'Excuse me, I'm a police officer. Are you … ' but Macleod got no further. As he was speaking, Finlay was turning around, removing his hands from his coat pockets. In each he held a pistol. Without any hesitation, Finlay shot Macleod in the chest with a single shot. Constable MacDonald, without thinking, dived towards Finlay, who fired a further two shots. The first bullet hit MacDonald in the upper right arm while the second entered his groin. He too, fell to the ground in agony.

Finlay began walking back in the direction from which he had come and glanced quickly at the two men on the ground as he walked briskly past them. Just at that moment, uniformed beat constable Charles Hill, who had heard the shots, emerged from Montague Lane onto Hyndland Road and quickly took in the scene. He recognised his colleagues lying on the ground and then saw Finlay slightly further away, still holding the pistols in his hands. Finlay immediately became aware of Hill's presence and began to run across Hyndland Road towards Westbourne Terrace. Hill, blowing his whistle to attract attention, gave chase. Members of the public and local residents, alerted by the sound of gunfire and the police whistle, now began arriving on the scene and attended, as best they could, to the two injured officers. Other residents rushed to telephone the police and very soon, squad cars with sirens blaring, were rushing to Hyndland Road. As constable Hill chased Finlay, the young man fired shots at his pursuer but all of them missed their target.

In the heat of the chase, Finlay made a mistake. He ran into Westbourne Terrace Lane South and found out very quickly that it was a dead end. Doors led off the lane, but each one he tried was firmly locked. He turned round and found his way blocked by constable Hill, who shouted to Finlay, 'Come on out. Don't bother firing anymore.' Finlay, resigned to the fact that he was trapped, retorted, 'Stand back. I'll get you anyway.' As Finlay prowled the lane, looking for an escape route, he continued to fire his pistols indiscriminately but regularly. Every 30 or 40 seconds a shot would ring out. Hill had taken cover behind a garden wall and took his cap, which he had been holding in his hand throughout the chase, and placed it on his baton. He then held it out from the line of the wall so that Finlay could see it clearly.

Hill then enticed Finlay by shouting, 'I can see you. Have a shot at that.' Finlay obliged and fired off three shots in quick succession, none of them hitting the target. Hill had done all of this on purpose. He had seen some of his colleagues, who had come to his assistance, at the window of one of the houses in the lane. He had lured Finlay into firing at his cap in order that his colleagues could pinpoint exactly where Finlay was in the lane. The other officers, by using resident's gardens, began to encroach on Finlay's hiding place. At some point, the young gunman must have heard them on the other side of the garden wall, for when a number of burly policemen burst into the lane through various doors, they were just in time to witness Finlay, sitting on the ground with his back propped against a wall and his pistol barrel placed tight against the side of his head. He looked towards the onrushing policemen as he pulled the trigger. Blood spattered up and across the faded whitewashed wall as the top half of Finlay's body slumped down to the ground. The short-lived siege was over.

Even although he had shot himself in the head at point-blank range, Finlay wasn't dead. An ambulance was summoned and he was quickly taken to the Western Infirmary, arriving there only minutes after the two constables he had shot, and who had been taken in a private taxicab that had been passing the scene and which had been commandeered by onlookers.

Edwin Finlay was pronounced dead on arrival at the hospital at 9.10pm. Constable Macleod died 20 minutes later. Constable MacDonald received treatment but his condition was considered critical. Doctors deemed that he was too weak to undergo surgery to remove the bullet from his groin and they were fighting to control the constant bleeding. It was almost a full week before it was successfully removed and MacDonald remained in hospital for almost a month.

Finlay's body was searched and the full extent of his arsenal became evident. Apart from the Spanish-made pistol he used to shoot himself, the .22 Beretta pistol was found in his coat pocket and the .38 Webley revolver was found in his trouser pocket. A bandolier of cartridges for all the weapons was strapped around his waist, while on his wrist was a miniature bandolier containing .22 ammunition. Also found in his pockets was over £100 in cash, travel ticket stubs for his jaunt to Dublin and the ticket for the left luggage department at St Enoch's railway station which was found to contain a three-figure sum when police retrieved it. As the newspaper headlines revealed the story over morning breakfast tables in the west of Scotland, most people were asking the same question. How and why had this been allowed to happen?

Police probed Finlay's background in great depth and found some interesting facts. Finlay had been a member of the Army Cadet Force and had been very experienced in handling all types of firearms. He was considered by senior army officers to be an expert marksman. Police maintained that if they had known about this from the start, they probably would not have sent out unarmed officers to intercept Finlay. Furthermore, there is no doubt that Finlay was infatuated with Ann Frier, and it was concluded that on that fateful Thursday night, he meant to meet up with her and ask her to go away with him. If she refused, he would have shot her dead and then fled, via St Enoch's railway station, stopping only to uplift his left luggage.

Constable Macleod was buried in the small cemetery at Aignish, on his native Isle of Lewis. Finlay was cremated on Tuesday 8th September at the Western Necropolis, Glasgow and his ashes scattered in the Garden of Remembrance there.

The Lord Provost of Glasgow set up a fund in memory of Constable Macleod. Within hours, the total had reached £1000, thanks mainly to a £500 donation from Hugh Fraser (later Sir), owner of the House of Fraser department stores. Money came to the fund from many quarters. Even the Scottish Football Association helped by organising football matches where the gate money was donated to the fund. By the end of 1952, the fund totalled in excess of £5000, most of which was given to Mrs Macleod and her four-year-old son.

Constable Macleod was posthumously awarded the British Empire Medal. His colleagues MacDonald and Hill received the same award. A civilian, Mr Robert Hamilton, who at one point during the siege in the lane, had lain beside Constable Hill to, as he had put it, 'keep him company', was awarded the Queen's Commendation for his bravery.

The case of how an 18-year-old youth came into possession of three unlicensed firearms was subsequently raised in the House of Commons and as a result, changes were later made to the firearms legislation, whereby possession of 'antique' firearms would require the granting of a firearms' certificate.

Chapter 21
Garnethill, October 1952

Constant autumn showers fell in Glasgow at the beginning of October 1952. Day after day, the rain fell relentlessly; the type of rain that Scots folk describe as 'small rain – the kind that soaks right through you'. Everything felt damp. Little Betty Alexander was four years old and lived with her parents at 43 Buccleuch Street in Glasgow's Garnethill area. Her mop of black curly hair made her instantly recognisable to all in the area. On the evening of Tuesday 7th October 1952, little Betty was allowed out to play in the street outside her home, with a couple of her friends. It was about five pm and this was not a normal habit but due to the rain children had been forced to remain indoors for many days. With a break in the weather, lots of children all over the city were allowed out to play for the first time in days.

About 6.30 that night, Mrs Alexander called for her daughter from the window of her first-floor flat. Betty didn't answer and was nowhere to be seen. Mrs Alexander then went into the street and began calling again but there was no reply. A couple of young girls, who knew Betty, stopped what they were doing and accompanied Mrs Alexander as she went from street to street looking for her daughter. After an hour and with still no sign of Betty, the police were notified that she had gone missing. A major search quickly swung into operation involving a street-by-street search by torchlight which also took in the myriad of lanes that ran through the district. Air raid shelters, backcourts and middens were all looked into by police, who were assisted by willing members of the public, which swelled the numbers searching, but it was all to no avail.

By first light on Wednesday morning, with no sign of the missing child, the uniform branch of Glasgow Police called in the detectives of the CID. Betty's description was circulated. She was known to have been wearing a fawn- and brown-coloured coat, a kilt, a grey, red and green coloured pullover and brown shoes. An even more intensive search was undertaken during the daylight hours of Wednesday. All outhouses, cellars and yards in the Garnethill area were visited as the search area widened. Even so, not one trace of little Betty was found. When news of her disappearance was revealed in the newspapers, the police were inundated with reports of possible sightings. One such report caused police to call on the manager of a large Sauchiehall Street store very late on the Wednesday night. When he opened up the premises, the police searched it thoroughly but found nothing.

All day Thursday was spent by some police officers searching and re-searching areas of interest while others were sifting through reports of possible sightings. But again, no real clues as to Betty's whereabouts were revealed.

On Friday afternoon, 10th October, just after two pm, the news came that no one wanted to hear. The body of a young girl had been found in the rear yard of the Royal Hospital for Sick Children Dispensary in West Graham Street. The yard of the premises was situated in Buccleuch Lane. The body had been found by a cleaner, who only had reason to go into the yard on a weekly basis. Betty's coat had been removed and then draped over two or three steps at the top of a flight of stairs. The little girl's body had then been placed on top of the coat. To those who witnessed the scene of the discovery, the little girl's clothing seemed in disarray, although there were no apparent visible injuries. It was thought that the little girl had been dead for a number of days and that her body had lain in its final position for the same length of time. The yard had not been checked by police during their searches because it was private property and had been securely locked. It was also surrounded by walls that were at least seven feet high. It was noted that there were no windows in any property overlooking the yard which was only 200 yards from the Alexander home.

Almost immediately, on word spreading through the district, a crowd quickly gathered at both ends of Buccleuch Lane. Within an hour, more than 1000 onlookers thronged the lane, held back by squads of policemen. Over the course of the weekend, with more than 40 detectives and even more uniformed officers working on the investigation, police interviewed almost 3000 people. From these statements, the police were able to piece together little Betty's movements and it was ascertained that she was last seen alive at 5.30pm on Tuesday evening in Buccleuch Street.

A postmortem was carried out over the weekend and the cause of death was declared as shock, brought on by being the victim of an assault. On Monday afternoon, Betty Alexander's funeral took place, starting at her home address. More than 5000 people, mainly women and children, stood outside in Buccleuch Street or lined the route. Some spectators had gathered four hours before the ceremony began and it made no difference to them that Glasgow experienced downpour after downpour of heavy rain throughout the entire day. The cortege left Garnethill and proceeded to the graveside in Cadder cemetery in Bishopbriggs.

Tuesday saw a major breakthrough in the murder case. A fingerprint was discovered near to where Betty's body had lain in the enclosed yard. The partial print was found on the lock mechanism of the metal gate at the entrance to the yard. At one point, police removed the entire gate from its mountings and took it away for further examination. A house attached to the yard where Betty's body had been found was searched. The house, which had lain empty for at least six weeks, revealed no clues whatsoever.

Police then took the unique step of asking every male resident over 17 years of age in the Garnethill area to voluntarily offer up their fingerprints to be compared against the prints held by them. The authorities issued the following statement: 'To assist in the investigation of this crime, the Chief Constable appeals to you, as a male of 17 years or over, to allow your finger-prints to be taken. It is to be clearly understood that you may refuse to have your fingerprints taken, but nevertheless the Chief Constable hopes that he will have your full co-operation and gives you an undertaking that these fingerprints will be duly used in connection with this inquiry and will be destroyed as soon as they have served that purpose.'

Again the police appealed for some of Betty's playmates to come forward to be interviewed. It is believed that at least one of her friends held vital infor-mation about the night she disappeared. The child the police were looking for was about five years of age, small, fair-haired and wore a black coat and shoes and a blue ribbon in her hair. Within hours of this appeal being broadcast, three little girls were taken by their parents to the Northern Police Headquarters to be interviewed by detectives. After the interviews, police intimated that they still sought further help.

At one press conference, police announced that two men and a woman were 'helping with inquiries'. After 13 hours of interviewing, the suspects were released. It turned out that they were a local family of husband, wife and teenage son and they had to be secreted out of the police station via a side door to avoid the crowd who had gathered outside the police office. They were then escorted by police back to their house, where a police guard remained at the close mouth. A statement regarding the family's involvement, or lack of it, was hurriedly made to the press so that the public did not get the wrong idea and end up taking matters into their own hands. Every night for a week since Betty's body was discovered crowds gathered nightly outside Northern Police Headquarters in Maitland Street and in Buccleuch Lane where the body was found. There was even a crowd gathered outside the Alexander's home in Buccleuch Street. On most nights, the crowds numbered in excess of 500 persons.

During the postmortem on Betty Alexander, a number of dog hairs were found on her body, sticking to her clothes. The police had taken samples of hair from every dog they could find in the Garnethill area. Very quickly, they were able to identify the dog and its owner, who stayed in a house just off Buccleuch Lane. However, they were able to discount this line of inquiry when it was realised that the dog must have come upon Betty's body while it had lain dead in the yard, sometime between the Tuesday night and the Friday afternoon discovery.

Almost two weeks had passed since the discovery of Betty Alexander's body when police confirmed that they had almost completed their mammoth task of fingerprinting all the male residents in the Garnethill district and were pleased to report that not one person had refused to provide his impressions. A miscalculation meant that police had ended up taking over 1000 sets of prints and not 700 as was originally intended.

Mrs Alexander, who had been out searching for her daughter on the night she had gone missing, told police in one of a number of statements that she made to them that she had seen what she thought was an ambulance parked outside the Sick Childrens' Dispensary entrance on West Graham Street. She saw a man standing beside the vehicle with what appeared to be a child in his arms, wrapped in a blanket. However, she did make a remark to her companions, who were assisting in the search, along the lines of, 'Look, there's another wee kiddie – and us looking for Betty.' However, when police made inquiries with the St Andrew's Ambulance service, they were told that there was no record of any ambulance being there on the night in question. The police believed that Mrs Alexander may have mistaken a brown van as an ambulance and they appealed for the driver of the vehicle to come forward. While the hunt for the van was ongoing, other police officers were hard at work, comparing the fingerprints of Garnethill residents with the partial fingerprint found at the scene of the murder. During the day, Mrs Alexander gave interviews to the newspapers. She stated that while searching for her daughter on Tuesday night, about eight pm, she heard a little girl calling, 'Mummy, mummy.' Mrs Alexander said this happened in Buccleuch Lane but when she went into the lane and called out, there was no answer.

Four weeks into the investigation police appealed for a man who had been seen in the company of two small girls in Buccleuch Lane on the night of Betty's disappearance, to come forward. Indeed, any person who saw the man was asked to contact police. Police also announced that they were now re-checking the 3000 or so statements already obtained in the inquiry. However, whether by accident or design, a high-ranking police officer was quoted in a daily newspaper stating that the police believed the murderer stayed within the Garnethill district and may have already been interviewed by police. The wanted man never came forward. Neither did anyone else.

Seven weeks into the inquiry two Glasgow detectives rushed north to Inverness-shire, where they were to interview a man who was already in custody on other matters. Within hours, the detectives were on their way home with nothing to show for their travels. The man, in custody on assault charges, had been drunk when arrested. In his inebriated condition, he had made remarks in relation to Betty Alexander's murder, which were conveyed to the officers working on the investigation. It turned out that the remarks were nothing more than the idle boasts of a drunk.

With that flurry of activity over, the case ground to a halt. No more appeals in newspapers, just the odd quote from a police spokesman to the effect that the inquiry still continued. All too soon, Christmas was upon the city's population and all thoughts turned to those closer to home.

Who killed Betty Alexander? Was it a local resident as the police thought? Certainly the body was dumped in a place where no one could see it. That fact alone could suggest knowledge of the locality but that knowledge did not necessarily have to belong to a local. Consider the fact that police took over 1000 sets of fingerprints of local men but failed to find a match to the ones lifted at the scene. The little girl was assaulted, but not sexually, and she died from the resultant shock. Could it be that the killer was a local woman? Could it be that the partial fingerprint belonged to a female? No women's fingerprints were ever requested by police.

It also has to be said, although it wasn't made public at the time, that quite a number of the detective officers involved in the investigation suspected Mrs Alexander herself! Their feelings came about because of the way she conducted herself during the inquiry. Police officers felt that the story of a little child crying, 'Mummy, mummy,' in Buccleuch Lane of all places, on the night Betty disappeared, was far too coincidental. The fact that Mrs Alexander did not mention this incident at all to the police until *after* Betty's body was found on the Friday afternoon, also strengthened their suspicions. If she had mentioned it before then, the police would have conducted a more intimate and detailed search of the Buccleuch Lane and this would have led to the discovery of Betty's body much sooner.

In any event, it was proved that Betty was killed elsewhere and placed in the yard in the lane, so Mrs Alexander could not have heard her daughter's call at that time. Police were also suspicious of her alleged sighting of a man carrying a child outside the Sick Children's Dispensary in West Graham Street. Checks proved that it could not have been an ambulance, nor was any child admitted or discharged from the hospital that night. Mrs Alexander's alleged remark of, 'Look, a wee kiddie. And us looking for Betty,' just seemed to police to be contrived.

As a consequence, Mrs Alexander sent the detectives off on a hunt for an imaginary vehicle – the brown van – when the resources could have been used elsewhere to greater effect. Far from being of assistance to the investigation into her daughter's murder, she impeded it. The killer of Elizabeth 'Betty' Alexander, aged four years, remains undetected to this day.

Chapter 22

- -
West George Street Lane, June 1956

Ellen Petrie was 48 years old and had experienced a lifetime of misery. After a difficult childhood growing up in Southport, Lancashire, without a father who had been killed serving in the forces in World War 1, her luck didn't change. Ellen married in 1936, to a man named Jackson and they went to live in Liverpool. Together, they had a son, but when he was four years old, both he and her husband were killed during a Luftwaffe air raid on Liverpool docks. Ellen moved north to Glasgow just after the end of the war, and in 1952 she met and married John Petrie. They went to live at 160 Curle Street in Whiteinch, which was convenient for her husband's work in the Singer sewing machine factory in Clydebank. Ellen's joy was short-lived however, when two years after they wed, her husband died suddenly.

Ellen flitted from one low-paid dead-end job to another in order to support herself. In June 1956, she found herself working in a women's hostel in Carrick Street, in the Anderston area of Glasgow. She was employed as a cleaner but occasionally helped out in the kitchen. It has to be stated that the hostel catered for women who 'were down on their luck'. Alcoholism was rife among the residents and the majority of them had turned to prostitution to pay for their addiction. Although Ellen Petrie held down a full-time job, she was no different from the rest of the women in the hostel; she was an alcoholic and a part-time prostitute. She had no real friends, only acquaintances, through her drinking habits and other nocturnal activities.

On the bright summer evening of Friday 15th June 1956, Ellen finished her work at the hostel just after seven pm and then called at one of the many local public houses in the area. This was situated in Argyle Street on the corner of Carrick Street. During her time in the pub, she met up with a number of the hostel's residents. She also made the acquaintance of a male, who bought her a drink. The male, who was later described as being well-dressed, between 40 and 50 years old, medium height with receding brown hair, didn't particularly stand out from the crowd. He laughed and joked with Ellen and some of her friends and bought her more alcohol.

During the time Ellen was in the bar, about two hours in total, she was

146

seen by a number of people who would later come forward as witnesses. Ellen was easy to remember on this particular night as she was wearing a vivid pink- and fawn-coloured check coat. Most of the witnesses remember seeing her in the bar, while one resident of the area took greater interest in Ellen's behaviour after she left the premises with her man friend.

About 9.10pm that night, Mrs Elizabeth Michael, a resident from Brown Street, was engaged in running an errand in the district when she spotted Ellen, her back against the wall of the pub with her partner pulled close to her. They were kissing each other, oblivious to the fact that they were the source of much delight and amusement to the many passers-by. Eventually, Ellen and her beau moved off and were seen again by Mrs Michael, about ten minutes later, when they were walking across Bothwell Street into Pitt Street. Another witness, 38-year-old Mrs Annie Burns, was in the company of Ellen during her time in the public house. They were drinking together in the general group but Burns did not pay any particular attention to the man who was Ellen's companion. Mrs Burns was to feature in subsequent events, in a manner that some people would construe as strange.

About 10.20pm that night, John McIlvenna, a worker in a bakery in West George Street, went to the back door of his premises to get some fresh air. When he opened it, he found Ellen Petrie lying on the doorstep. She was covered in blood and moaning quietly. McIlvenna thought that the woman was trying to say something but he could not hear what she was saying. He bent down closer to her but still could not make sense of her whispering. McIlvenna ran to the end of West George Street Lane and asked the first person he met to go and call for an ambulance. It was Mrs Annie Burns and she did as she was told and summoned some medical assistance. She then returned to the lane and ventured down it to where McIlvenna stood. Burns recoiled in horror when she saw Ellen Petrie lying on the ground in a large pool of blood with her distinctive coat heavily stained and discoloured with that blood. Petrie was lying on her back, her skirt lifted up and twisted around her waist. A shoe and a nylon stocking were both missing from her right leg and this is what drew Annie Burns' attention to the large 'V' shaped wound on the inside of her exposed upper right thigh.

By the time the ambulance arrived, Ellen Petrie was dead. Her life had slowly ebbed away in the deserted lane, watched over by a man she didn't know. Annie Burns had long since left the scene. The police arrived and two uniformed beat officers attended at first. As soon as they had observed the scene, they closed off the lane and called for the detectives. By the time CID officers arrived, it was dark, so they began a torchlight search of the lane, a plot of vacant ground adjacent to it and the small rear yard attached to St Columba's Church in St Vincent Street. The search yielded no clues whatsoever.

McIlvenna was interviewed. He really couldn't add much to the fact that he had found the body, although he mentioned the fact that Annie Burns had been present and had recognised the dead woman. She had even remarked that she had been drinking with her just an hour beforehand. But Burns had failed to provide a name for the dead woman before disappearing. As the police trawled the lane for clues, they also issued a description of the murdered woman to the newspapers and appealed for help in identifying her. They did state that they believed that she had been known as 'English Nellie'. This information came about as a consequence of Ellen Petrie's part-time occupation. One of the police officers at the scene recognised her from having previous dealings with her but could not remember her name. However, he was able to say that she was known by the street name of 'English Nellie' and that she used to reside in Curle Street in the Whiteinch area of the city.

When Annie Burns fled the scene, she had gone to a friend's home in nearby Garnethill. After telling her story, Annie offered to go to a chemist to get medicine for her friend's sick daughter. The offer was accepted and Burns left the house. On reaching Sauchiehall Street, Burns is alleged to have flagged down a passing vehicle, in this case, a van. She climbed in and set off. Within 200 yards, at the junction of Rose Street, the van collided with a bus and both Burns and the van driver were removed to the local infirmary, seriously injured. As a consequence of her accident, police did not get to interview Annie Burns until after the weekend when she had been discharged from hospital.

Over the course of that first weekend, police identified 'English Nellie' as Ellen Petrie, who had been residing at 76 Hill Street, Garnethill, in Glasgow. Numerous witnesses came forward and told of their involvement with Petrie. The police then broadcast an appeal for a man they wished to interview, to come forward. He had been seen in Ellen Petrie's company prior to her death and had also been seen by one witness running out of the lane just minutes before baker McIlvenna raised the murder alarm. No one came forward. Initially, police refused to discuss the injuries Ellen Petrie that had caused her death, other than to say that they were actively looking for a knife. Eventually, police were forced to admit that Petrie had bled to death from a wound on her thigh.

All weekend, detectives visited public houses in the Anderston area, trying to build up a picture of the movements of Ellen Petrie on the night of her death. They also visited cafés, snooker halls, cinemas and coffee stalls, trying to find out any snippet of information. The only thing that did come to light was that the police were now linking the murder of Ellen Petrie with two other similar attacks on women in the general area, which had occurred in the previous eight weeks. One night, near the end of April, Mrs Margaret Davies was attacked and severely injured in Brown Street. Mrs Davies, or 'Ginger Margaret' as she was known in the district, had been out on a 'date' with a man she had met once before. He had walked her to her home, the women's hostel in Carrick Street (where Ellen Petrie worked), and as she walked away from him, he called her back. She turned and walked back and on reaching him, he punched her full on the face, knocking her to the ground. The man produced a knife and began slashing at her body and throat.

As the man hacked at her skirt to try and get to her legs underneath, Davies managed to get to her feet and run off. She eventually reached the sanctuary of the hostel and an ambulance was called. It was at this time that 'Ginger Margaret' realised how badly she had been injured and she needed 25 stitches inserted into her wounds at the hospital. Police were given a description of her attacker.

Then, at the start of June, in Robertson Street, just two streets away from Brown Street, and two weeks before Petrie's murder, 31-year-old Ina McDonald was attacked and assaulted. Mrs McDonald had met a man in a local public house and was walking with him in Robertson Street when, without any warning, he pulled her into a derelict close mouth and began attacking her. The man began slashing and stabbing her. McDonald could only scream as the frenzied attack continued. Eventually, residents of Robertson Street investigated the woman's screams and came upon Mrs McDonald lying badly injured on a staircase landing area. Blood oozed from her many wounds, including her slashed throat. McDonald was rushed to hospital, where the medical staff fought to save her life. For a few days it was touch and go but she survived. Indeed, she was still in hospital receiving treatment when Ellen Petrie was attacked and murdered.

The wounds inflicted on all three women were very similar, especially in relation to the thigh wounds, which police tried very hard to keep secret; all they would say was that they were looking for an extremely sharp-bladed weapon. Each had injuries to the inside area of a thigh and each female had had her throat slashed. Medical opinion was that if the femoral artery had been severed, death would have occurred within two minutes due to loss of blood. So, it is possible that when baker McIlvenna opened his back door and found Ellen Petrie bleeding to death and trying to tell him something, the man responsible for her fatal injuries was still in the lane.

The description of the man who attacked 'Ginger Margaret' also matched that of Ina McDonald's assailant and both were identical to that of the male seen in Ellen Petrie's company. Even so, police had no name for this suspect. 'Ginger Margaret' was tracked down and interviewed by newspaper reporters. She was quoted as saying that all the women in the hostel were scared to go out at night as they believed that there was a maniac out to get them. With the previous two attacks remaining unsolved, the murder of Ellen Petrie went the same way within a few weeks. The investigation eventually came to a standstill because there was nowhere else to go with it. During those weeks when the inquiry was active, additional uniformed police officers were drafted into the Anderston area, in an effort to both try and catch the male responsible and to reassure the female members of the population.

After about two weeks of the extra patrols, complaints were made about how it was affecting businesses in the area. Public houses and cinemas openly declared that they were experiencing a downturn in business and were very unhappy about it all. Complaints were also made, albeit quietly, from those engaged in the oldest of professions, that their clients were being chased away.

The circumstances of Annie Burns being at the end of the lane when a drinking associate of hers was being murdered would seem to most people to be much more than a coincidence. It certainly seemed that way to the police investigating the case. They were of the opinion that Burns was waiting there to be joined by Ellen Petrie after the latter had completed a 'piece of business' in the lane with the man from the pub. The fact that Burns did not see the man exit the lane is due simply to the fact he left by the other end.

In 1958, Peter Anthony Manuel, the Lanarkshire serial killer, a few days before he was executed for his crimes, allegedly admitted that he was responsible for Ellen Petrie's murder. He was never interviewed at any great length about this admission and when his photograph was shown to both Ina McDonald and 'Ginger' Margaret Davies, they failed to identify him as their attacker.

It has to be said that the descriptions given by both women at the time of their attacks, and by witnesses in the Petrie case of the man seen in her company over the course of the night of her murder, could have fitted that of Manuel, but with one exception. All the descriptions stated that the wanted man was between 40 and 50 years of age but Manuel was only 29 years old at the time of the killing.

One other fact that should be considered is the use of the particular modus operandi in the three attacks. Prior to April 1956, when 'Ginger' Margaret was attacked, Manuel had assaulted other women with a knife but had never injured any of them by gouging a 'V' shape wound in their thigh. It is very strange to think that he only used this particular method over a short period of time in 1956 and then never used it again.

If Manuel can be discounted many questions are raised. Why did this murderer select only prostitutes? Was it because he considered them an easy target? They had all been drinking, some might say excessively, so it follows that any resistance to his attacks would be easier to overcome. Did he hate these women, purely because they were prostitutes? There were no more attacks or murders of women using similar methods. But why was this? Did the police presence and investigation come too close to him that he decided to stop? Did he move away or was he imprisoned? Did he simply die?

Or did he turn his attentions to another sector of the community? All these questions remain unanswered to this day.

Chapter 23
Lanarkshire, 1956-8

If the question of who was Scotland's most evil man was posed, then it is certain that some of the following would feature. Burke and Hare (either together or separately), Bible John (whoever he was), and in a different sense, Aleister Crowley. But for the sheer ability to terrorise a population, then the accolade, if that is the right word, must go to Peter Anthony Manuel. In the late 1950s, whole communities on the outskirts of the south side of Glasgow were terrified to go to sleep. Some families made at least one member of the household stay awake through the night while others ran up larger than usual electricity bills by keeping lights on 24 hours a day. It is a well-known fact that almost every hardware store in Glasgow sold out of locks, door chains and other security devices.

Thousands of words have been written about the theory of whether criminals are born or bred. It can be fairly assumed that Manuel was one of the latter. In his early teens, he first came to the notice of the law, which resulted in him being sent to borstal. But rather than it being a deterrent, it was, in effect, an academy of criminal learning.

Manuel was born in New York in 1927 after his parents had emigrated to the USA. But they had swapped depression-hit central Scotland for similar circumstances in a foreign country. Within five years, they had returned to the UK, settling this time in Coventry. Before he was 19, Manuel had escaped from ten different institutions where he had been sent for a variety of crimes, ranging from shop-breaking to robbery with violence, to indecent assault. As early as March 1946, Manuel was responsible for assaults on women in the south side of Glasgow and its surroundings. One of the incidents involved him assaulting, abducting and raping a woman from Bothwell. She told Manuel that she had only been released from hospital after a serious illness two weeks previously, but still he persisted with his attack.

Three women had been attacked within the space of a week. All gave descriptions of the attacker which in parts fitted that of Manuel. The day following the last attack (the rape), Manuel was detained and put on an identification parade at the local police office. One victim positively identified him, while the second looked straight at him but before she could say anything, she fainted and had to be carried out of the room. The rape victim surprisingly did not identify Manuel, although, of the three, she was the one who had spent the most time in his company. At the time of the identification parade, Manuel was on bail for housebreaking. Very soon after, he was found guilty of this charge and 14 other similar charges and sentenced to 12 months' imprisonment.

This was a break for the authorities and the locus of the rape was examined in minute detail by the police forensic scientists. Slowly but methodically, they were able to collect enough evidence that led to Manuel being tried and convicted of the rape. He was sentenced to eight years, which was to start at the end of his current 12-month sentence. From his prison cell, Manuel protested that he was innocent of the charge to no avail. Instead, Manuel retreated into himself in prison and was considered by the prison authorities to be very much a loner. He was released early in 1955 and returned to his family home in Uddingston. Almost immediately, he became involved with Anne O'Hara, a bus conductress from Carluke. He had met her while travelling to work on her bus every morning. After a couple of months' courtship, they became engaged and a date for the wedding was set for 30thJuly 1955. It never took place.

For reasons best known to himself, Manuel wrote Anne O'Hara an anonymous letter, spelling out his criminal past and stating that he worked for the Secret Service. Not surprisingly, O'Hara broke off the engagement. Whether by design or accident, Manuel chose the date of his cancelled wedding to attack another female, this time in Lucie Brae, Birkenshaw, Lanarkshire.

Mary McLaughlin, a 29-year-old from the village, was returning late at night from a dance in nearby Blantyre. She got off the bus and began walking up the darkened brae when she felt a knife being pressed against her throat. She managed to scream once, her second being stifled by Manuel's hand, before being pushed and dragged across a wall and into a field. Her scream had been heard by a number of people, including two policemen, but a search of the area by them revealed nothing. McLaughlin and Manuel lay in the field all night, talking and smoking cigarettes. Manuel made no attempt to rape her, although at one stage he did sexually assault her. At one point, in an effort to gain her confidence, Manuel threw his knife away over a railway embankment.

By the light of the matches and cigarettes, McLaughlin recognised her attacker as someone who had shared the same morning bus on her way to work. However, she did not let on to Manuel about this and she was eventually able to convince him that if he were to let her go, she would not report the matter. Manuel agreed and somewhat strangely, escorted her home. McLaughlin immediately contacted the police and Manuel was arrested and charged without delay. He went on trial in October of that year at Airdrie Sheriff Court. For the first time, he was to show himself off to a greater audience than his victims. He defended himself, using knowledge he had gained during his many incarcerations. Such were his skills, he was able to convince the jury to return a not proven verdict. Once more, Manuel was free to roam.

Just as it was getting dark on the late afternoon of 4th January 1956, George Gribbon was walking on the golf course at East Kilbride, looking to see if he could find lost golf balls. As he walked by the side of the 5th hole he saw what appeared to be a body lying in the undergrowth. It turned out to be that of 17-year-old local girl Annie Knielands. She had met a horrific and frenzied end with her skull smashed into at least 15 pieces. Her body also carried a large number of cuts, thought to have come from barbed wire fencing nearby. Annie Knielands had left her home on 2nd January in order to meet the local bus. Her new boyfriend had arranged to meet her there, after having been introduced at the New Year. For one reason or another he had failed to keep the appointment and it is thought that she met her killer at the bus stop as she waited. All known criminals were visited by the police and Manuel's turn came ten days after the discovery of the body. He simply stated that on the night in question, he never left his house. This was corroborated by his parents.

One interesting point is that at the time of his interview, Manuel was sporting a number of scratches on both his nose and right cheek. When asked about them, he calmly stated that he had received them in a fight in Glasgow city centre on Hogmanay, although he could not provide a description for his assailant. With nothing to go on, the murder enquiry plodded on, with Manuel free to carry on with his nocturnal wanderings as and when he pleased.

On the night of 23rd March, torchlights bounced off the canteen building of Hamilton Colliery. Almost as the jemmy was placed into the doorframe, a dozen policemen came running from the shadows and one would-be housebreaker was arrested at the scene whilst the other managed to get away. No matter, he had been recognised and within a few hours, Peter Manuel was dragged from his bed, put in handcuffs and taken to Hamilton Police Station. He appeared in court the next day, where, despite his already lengthy record, he was granted bail and trial was set for seven months in the future (October).

Two weeks before his trial began, the last few chapters in Manuel's grotesque life of crime began to unfold. He decided to break into the house of William Watt at 5 Fennsbank Avenue, Burnside. Mr Watt was a baker to trade and owned five bakery shops. Rightly or wrongly, Manuel considered that the house would hold a large sum of money, hopefully the takings from the shops.

Manuel also had information that the occupants at 18 Fennsbank Avenue were away on holiday and he decided to break into this house first as a 'dry run'. It went according to plan although the proceeds only amounted to a couple of pieces of jewellery and a small amount of cash. Nonetheless, it was all about the larger target at No 5 Fennsbank Avenue. Unbeknown to Manuel, Watt had left a couple of days beforehand and gone on a fishing holiday to Argyllshire. In his absence, the likelihood of there being large sums of cash takings in the house was almost non-existent.

In the small hours of 17th September, a pane in the front door was smashed, allowing the latch to be released. Manuel entered the house and moved quickly along the hallway. He came to the master bedroom and pushed the door quietly open. He then approached the bed, where he could see two people sleeping. Without warning, he produced a Webley .45 calibre pistol and took careful aim at one of the figures sleeping in the bed. The sound of the shot seemed to echo around the room and beyond. The bullet entered the skull of the figure in the bed. Death for the 45-year-old invalid Marion Watt was instantaneous. As Manuel took in the scene, the second figure in the bed sat upright. Manuel never hesitated as he fired his second shot, which once again entered the head of his victim. Margaret Brown, sister of Marion, fell backwards onto her pillow.

Manuel moved closer to the bed and looked down on the two women. Both were dead but he wasn't finished yet. He stood over the body of Margaret Brown, slowly took careful aim once more and fired another bullet into his victim's head. With the third gunshot, 16-year-old Vivienne Watt awoke and ran out of her bedroom to see what had caused the commotion. At the same time, Manuel heard her and ran into the hallway. As Vivienne rushed and stumbled in the darkness, Manuel lashed out at the young girl and caught her flush on the chin with a punch, which knocked her unconscious. He picked her up and carried her back into her room, where he placed her on the bed.

Manuel then sat on the end of the bed and casually lit up a cigarette. As he smoked, Vivienne slowly began to regain consciousness. Her attacker feigned concern and his attempts to comfort her met with a rebuff from the young girl. Not one to take rejection easily, Manuel threw her down onto the pillow and cruelly shot her in the head. What happened after this to the three women is a prime example of Manuel's depravity. All three were arranged in positions on the bed where their genitalia were exposed, although no sexual assault was committed on them. It would seem that Manuel found it necessary to dominate and humiliate them, even when they were dead.

Later that morning, about 8.45am, the Watt's daily help, Mrs Collinson arrived and found the front door ajar. She called out to the occupants but did not receive any reply. Just then, the postman came down the driveway and entered the house. He quickly discovered the scene of carnage and called for the police. Amazingly, Vivienne was still alive at this time, although she could not speak. Unfortunately, she only survived another 20 minutes until just before the police arrived.

As the murder enquiry swung into action, some vital evidence was discovered; a cigarette end and a burn mark on the carpet near to Vivienne's bed. Detectives were aware that Peter Manuel had two idiosyncrasies; one was opening tins of food and pouring the contents over furniture and the other was smoking a cigarette while sitting somewhere like the edge of a bed and then stubbing it out on the carpet. At 18 Fennsbank Avenue, the bed had been lain in, a tin of tomato soup had been tipped over the carpet in the living room and a cigarette end stubbed out on it also.

Within hours, police officers raided Manuel's house, but nothing came of it. They even searched his house four days later, again with a negative result. Very soon the police turned their suspicions in another direction.

Mr Watt became a suspect, even though he had been at least 90 miles away in Argyllshire. Somehow the police decided that he had the time to drive from his hotel to his home, murder his family and then drive back again, all in good time. It was accepted that the journey from Argyllshire to Glasgow took at least two hours. Glasgow Police recreated the journey, using an experienced driver from the Traffic Department and managed to do it in two hours and five minutes. This therefore 'proved' that a return journey could have been done on the night of the murder.

The newspapers were full of all the latest reports and this caused 'witnesses' to come forward. One, John Taylor, the ferry master of the Erskine Ferry across the Clyde, went to the police and was able to identify Watt, his car and his dog, as being on his ferry in the early morning of the murders, crossing from the Dumbarton side to the south side. William Watt was arrested and charged with the murders of his wife, daughter and his sister-in-law. He was remanded in custody and sent to Barlinnie Prison on 27th September 1956. Unwittingly, the authorities then rubbed salt into the wounds of an innocent man. Peter Manuel was soon to become an inmate of Barlinnie, after being sentenced to a term of 18 months imprisonment for the Hamilton Colliery canteen job. He wasted no time in seeking out Watt and striking up a 'friendship' with the confused man.

All Manuel needed to do was sit back, do his time and keep his mouth shut. It looked as if an innocent man was about to be found guilty of one of his crimes. But that was not in Manuel's make-up. He asked Watt's solicitor, Lawrence Dowdall, to visit him in jail. Manuel told Dowdall that his client was innocent and that he knew who the killer was. Over the course of three interviews, Dowdall cleverly allowed Manuel to talk, almost uninterrupted, and it became obvious to the lawyer that Manuel knew too much detail not to have been involved himself, no matter how much he blamed others.

Eventually, after much petitioning, the Crown Office dropped the charges against Mr Watt and on 3rd December 1956, 67 days after his arrest, the baker was released from his prison cell.

But it still wasn't over.

Manuel walked out of the gates of Barlinnie into the early morning frost of 30th November 1957. The first thing he did was telephone Watt and arranged to meet him. All told, Manuel and Watt met three times in as many days. On each occasion, Manuel blamed others for the killings without actually naming anyone and there is evidence to suggest that Manuel was trying to get Watt to give him money in return for his 'information'. Mr Watt always denied that he had ever paid Manuel anything.

Manuel abruptly left the Glasgow area in the following week and turned up in Newcastle, where he applied, and was interviewed, for a job. At Newcastle railway station, about 4.30am on the 7th December 1957, Manuel climbed into a waiting taxi at the rank outside and instructed the driver to take him to Edinburgh. The following day the taxi was found abandoned on the high moors of County Durham near Edmondbyers. It looked like an abandoned wreck, with all its windows and lights smashed and its doors lying open. The body of 36-year-old taxi driver Sydney Dunn was lying over 100 yards away; he had been shot in the back of the head and his throat had been slashed. The police believed he had been murdered because he simply took a wrong turning on the way to Edinburgh.

The next time Manuel committed a crime was in the early hours of Christmas Day. He broke into a house at 66 Western Road, Mount Vernon,

Glasgow but his haul was sparse – a camera, £2 in cash and a pair of sheepskin gloves. Manuel had the affront to parcel up the stolen items and present them to his father and sister as Christmas gifts. On Saturday 28th December, Manuel continued with his murderous behaviour. Isabelle Cooke, a 17-year-old from Carrick Drive in Mount Vernon, was waiting at a bus stop in Uddingston for her boyfriend to arrive. This incidentally was the same location where 11 years beforehand, Manuel had attacked a mother and child.

Once again, Manuel took a victim at a bus stop. He abducted Isabelle, sexually assaulted her and murdered her before burying her semi-nude body in a shallow grave in a field next to the old Baillieston Brickworks. Her worried parents reported Isabelle as missing the following day. An extensive search was mounted by police during which some of the young girl's clothing was found in a river, while her handbag was found in a local colliery shaft. Even as the search for Isabelle continued, Manuel's thirst for blood continued.

A few hours after the bells had brought in the New Year of 1958, Manuel was back on the prowl, again in Uddingston. He broke into the home of Peter and Doris Smart and their 11-year-old son, Michael. He shot each of them once in the head, killing all of them outright. However, the strangest part of Manuel's behaviour was not revealed until police had interviewed all the witnesses. A neighbour noted that the curtains of the Smart's bungalow were closed on New Year's Day, but the following day the postman was able to say that some curtains were open when he called at 10.30am The dustman then stated that all curtains were closed at two pm on the same day. The same postman passed by the next morning (3rd January) and this time all the curtains were open. Once again, by two pm that afternoon, a neighbour reported that all the curtains were closed. Later that day, about six pm, the same neighbour saw the curtains open, lights on within the house and the Smart's car, an Austin A35 in the driveway.

The following day, it was reported that only the living room curtains were open along with two small windows at the front, yet by the same afternoon, all the curtains were closed again. The next day, Sunday 5th January, nothing unusual was noticed, probably because it was the quietest day of the week.

On Monday morning, police in the Gorbals area of Glasgow received a report of an abandoned car in Florence Street. It turned out to be the Smart's Austin A35. The car's registration led the police to Uddingston and when two police officers forced their way into the house, they found the three corpses. The detectives who followed them also found biscuits in the kitchen sink and an opened tin of salmon. The murder inquiry then got a break when an informant told them that Manuel appeared to be flush with money and when checks were made, it was found that the notes Manuel had passed were crisp and new. Further investigations revealed that the banknotes matched those stolen from the Smart's house.

Police raided Manuel's home and seized his clothes for forensic examination. During the search, a pair of sheepskin gloves and a Kodak camera were also seized. Manuel's sister, Theresa, and his father, Samuel, gave statements detailing how they received them as Christmas gifts from Peter Manuel. Manuel was arrested and taken to Bellshill Police Station, where he was eventually charged with breaking into the house at Western Road, Mount Vernon and stealing a pair of sheepskin gloves, a camera and £2 in cash. He was kept in custody.

The following day, Manuel was put on an identity parade and picked out by numerous witnesses who had accepted the stolen money in various pubs and hotels. As a result, Manuel was charged with the Smart's murders. As Manuel languished in custody, he had plenty of time to ponder on what his next move was to be. He decided quickly on his course of action. Manuel asked to speak with detectives and offered to tell them about unsolved local crimes, particularly murders, on the condition that he was allowed to speak with his mother and father first.

His request was agreed to and at the meeting, Manuel told his parents, 'There's no future for me. I have done some terrible things. I killed the girl Knielands at East Kilbride and I shot the three women in the house at Bothwell.' The meeting lasted about half and hour, after which Manuel kept his promise to reveal his actions. He went on to write a confession to the murder of Isabelle Cooke.

Just after midnight a convoy of cars and vans arrived at the field at the side of Baillieston Brickworks and Manuel was allowed to walk up and down the field in an effort to locate the grave of his victim. After much debate, probably due to the field having been ploughed since the murder, Manuel, handcuffed, indicated with his foot and coldly said, 'I think she is there. I think I am standing on her.' How right he was. Nine inches below the surface, as the earth was gently removed by the shovels of two uniformed officers, Isabelle Cooke's decomposing corpse was exposed to the frosty night air.

Back at the police office, Manuel gave the detective officers information on what he had done with the guns he had used in the murders of both the Watt and the Smart families. He had thrown them both in the River Clyde.

Police frogmen were to later recover them easily, thanks to the precise information given by Manuel. Indeed, the Webley pistol used in the Watt murders was located beneath the Suspension Bridge at Carlton Place in less than half and hour.

Manuel wrote further full confessions to the Watt murders, the Annie Knielands murder and finally the Smart murders and was eventually charged with a total of eight murders, three house-breakings and the theft of Mr Smart's car. He went on trial at Glasgow High Court on 12th May 1958 before Lord Cameron. The jury was quickly selected and sworn in. It consisted of nine men and six women. Every day for the duration of the trial, hundreds of people waited for hours for the chance to get a seat in the public gallery and every day hundreds of people were turned away. They didn't leave the area, preferring instead to loiter outside the court buildings, waiting on any snippet of news from inside. Even newspaper reporters fought over the seating arrangements.

The newspapers carried daily reports that were also transmitted around the world, such was the interest that Manuel generated. After nine days of evidence, Manuel sensationally sacked his defence team and began defending himself. The most significant part of this was that he was able to personally cross-examine William Watt when the latter gave evidence in the case. Manuel tried very hard to give Watt an uncomfortable time in the witness box. He shouted, sometimes rambling on at length, not even asking a question at the end of it all and even occasionally tried to ridicule the older man. Watt stood his ground and failed to be intimidated.

After this, reports suggest that Manuel began to accept that the inevitable was about to happen. He slumped and slouched in the dock where once he had sat ramrod straight. He stared straight ahead for long periods and his hands quivered, although he tried hard to hide this by grabbing hold of the side of his trouser legs.

The jury retired to consider their verdict. It wasn't long before they were back. They found Manuel not guilty of Annie Knielands murder, as they had been directed to by the judge, due to lack of corroborative evidence and also not guilty to one of the housebreakings. On all the other charges, including six of capital murder, the jury returned guilty verdicts.

There could be no other sentence. Manuel stood solemnly as the macer of the court moved silently behind the judge and the black triangular hat was placed on the judge's head momentarily. Lord Cameron read out the following: 'Peter Thomas Anthony Manuel, in respect of the verdict of guilty of capital murder and of murder done on a different occasion, the sentence of this court is that you be taken from this place to the prison of Barlinnie, Glasgow, therein detained until the 19th day of June next, and upon that day in the said prison of Barlinnie, Glasgow, and between the hours of eight and ten o'clock, you suffer death by hanging, which is pronounced for doom.'

Manuel appealed his sentence but it was rejected and a new date – 11th July – was set for his execution. It was reported by newspapers that just after receiving this information, Manuel was rushed to the prison hospital as he had swallowed a large quantity of bleach but it was not that strong and he quickly recovered. However, two prison officers were now detailed to watch the prisoner's every move, 24 hours a day.

More recent information suggests that this attempt at suicide did not take place, as it wasn't Manuel's 'style'. Instead, in the three weeks after his appeal had been turned down, Manuel said nothing nor smoked any of his cigarettes. He became totally withdrawn, sitting on his bed and staring at walls for long periods of time. He was attempting to feign insanity to the authorities for obvious reasons. However, his plan did not work and just as suddenly as he had begun this behaviour, two days before his execution he reverted to his old self, talking and smoking as if he had not a care in the world.

The morning of Friday 11th July 1958 dawned, bright and sunny. Manuel was in the execution cell and at one minute past eight the executioner entered, pinned Manuel's arms to his side and walked him across the corridor and into the execution chamber. His legs were pinioned and a white hood placed over his head. As all the men stepped back from the platform, the lever was pulled and Manuel dropped like a stone. It had all taken less than 30 seconds.

In the two days prior to his execution, Manuel admitted to the authorities that he had committed at least another three unsolved murders. In 1954, he strangled a Pimlico prostitute in London named Helen Carlin, then battered a 55-year-old woman, Anne Steele, to death. His last confession was to a murder that took place between the deaths of Annie Knielands and the Watt family. In June 1956, he claimed to have stabbed Ellen Petrie to death in Glasgow. (This is discussed in greater detail in Chapter 22).

Manuel never stood trial for the murder of Newcastle taxi driver Sydney Dunn. He couldn't be tried in Scotland for a crime that had occurred in England. On 28th July 1958, a coroner's court ruled that Mr Dunn had been murdered by Manuel, who himself was now dead.

A lot has been written previously of the supposed motives for Manuel's killings. Suffice to say that some of the theories require years of training in the field of psychiatry before being able to understand them. This author goes along with the simple explanation, given by the trial judge, Lord Cameron, who said that 'every once in a while, someone like Peter Thomas Anthony Manuel comes along who is mad, bad and dangerous.'

Chapter 24

Glasgow Green, January 1958, October 1959, January 1960

A middle-aged married couple were on their usual Sunday morning walk through Glasgow Green on their way to church on the cold and frosty morning of 26th January 1958. Their regular route took them past the park's imposing bandstand, but on this particular morning their stroll was harshly interrupted when they came upon the dead body of man, lying on a tarmac path that led to and from the bandstand. The body, of a man in his 40's, was lying on its side, with one arm outstretched and entangled on railings that ran alongside the path. The pool of blood that had gathered under the upper part of the body, looked as if it had frozen due to the bitterly cold weather.

The police were quickly on the scene and sealed off the area. The body was seen to have suffered serious face and head injuries, suggesting that the man had been beaten to death, but at this time, no formal cause of death could be established. The body was removed from the site and taken away for a postmortem examination, the result of which was that death had been as a consequence of a very deep stab wound to the neck.

With the body removed, the police examined the scene in greater detail. One of the first things the they had to establish was exactly where the crime had taken place. Had the man been assaulted elsewhere then staggered and stumbled to where he was found, or had he been attacked at his place of death? The first thing noticed was a lack of bloodstains anywhere in the vicinity, leading to the conclusion that the fatal attack had happened where the body had been found. Despite a search of a large area of parkland, bushes and nearby riverbank, no weapons were discovered.

An unusual feature of this case is that the dead man was quickly identified by some of the police officers who first attended the scene. His name was John Wilson Orr, nicknamed 'Ginger', a 40-year-old occasional newsvendor when he wasn't being a petty crook. He was estranged from his wife and child, possibly because he had spent the last 12 months in Barlinnie Prison, serving an 18-month sentence for housebreaking. He had been released from prison just before nine am on Saturday morning (25th January) and now police wanted to trace all of his movements since then. Once reports of the murder circulated and appeared in the newspapers, a number of people came forward and spoke with the police. Very quickly, a picture of Orr's movements on the Saturday were built up.

He is known to have called at the offices of the National Assistance Board in Reid Street, Bridgeton, where he collected some benefit money due to him. From then until about ten pm on Saturday night, Orr seems to have been in many people's company in a number of licensed premises in and around the Glasgow Cross/Bridgeton area. After ten pm, Orr's movements were practically unknown, although police did look to interview a number of youths, both boys and girls, who were seen in Glasgow Green near St Andrew's suspension bridge just after ten pm on Saturday night. They were heard to continually shout, 'John, John.' When traced, the youths explained that they had been shouting on a friend and had seen nothing of John 'Ginger' Orr that fateful night.

Eventually, after a couple of days, more pieces of John Orr's movements on his final night fell into place and his activities were accounted for right up to one am on the Sunday morning, about eight hours before his body was found. The police formed the opinion that this was around the time that Orr met his killer. The police were anxious to trace two persons who were seen in the company of Orr earlier on Saturday evening, but who had so far failed to come forward. One was a shabbily dressed man, about the same age and build as Orr. They were seen together in the Saltmarket area, near to Glasgow Green just after nine pm They were also looking to speak to a 25-year-old blonde woman who was with Orr in a café in Howard Street about 10.30pm. Orr and the woman had quite a loud argument there, during which the woman left. Despite appeals in the newspapers, neither of these witnesses made themselves known to the murder squad detectives.

Within a week, the murder inquiry had come to a halt. No further information was coming in. Orr's murder remains unsolved.

•　　•　　•

Richard Gibson was a 48-year-old casual worker who lived in a model lodging-house in Drygate, just off the High Street in Glasgow. He had a succession of short-term menial jobs and was, at that time, employed as porter in a city-centre hotel. He was described by those who knew him as a quiet and shy man. So how did he come to be lying on a tow-path of the river Clyde, on a bleak rainy Saturday morning in October 1959, stabbed to death?

The path, which starts in Glasgow Green and continues to Shawfield, was well used by those who knew of its existence and it was a workman on his way to a local factory that Saturday morning who came upon Gibson's corpse about seven am. It was lying half on, half off the path, partially obscured by the long grass at the side of the pathway. The workman summoned the police who attended and sealed off the scene. Detectives were seen to be coming and going all morning.

Uniformed officers spent most of the time controlling crowds of curious onlookers who had gathered on a bridge over the river which had a view of the incident. The body had been covered over with a large blue tarpaulin. When some of the crowd began jeering at the police activities below them, the decision was taken to clear the bridge of all spectators and this exclusion zone was maintained until the police completed their inquiries at the scene.

Police began an extensive search of the riverbank on both sides, from Shawfield Stadium to Hutchestown Bridge at the High Court Buildings at the foot of the Saltmarket. Long grass, reeds and bushes were cut back as the police searched for a weapon. Somewhat surprisingly, the police failed to drag the river at the murder scene, although the body was found only 20 yards from the water. It was soon discovered that Gibson had died as a result of being stabbed on the body and the neck several times. From the lack of a blood trail, police surmised that Gibson died at the place where he was attacked.

Police could only speculate the motive behind the killing as Gibson's wallet was found in his jacket pocket with its contents undisturbed. Within the wallet, police discovered the stub of a ticket for the performance of a show at the Pavilion Theatre the previous night. His seat was No 17, Row A in the balcony for the first house show. When police made inquiries at the theatre in Renfield Street, they found a member of staff who remembered seeing Gibson and she was adamant that the victim had been alone.

Police were severely disappointed in the response to their appeal for information on Gibson's movements on Friday night. Apart from his attendance at the theatre, nothing is known of his subsequent activities or how he came to be on a pathway of the Clyde as it ran through Glasgow Green. All too soon, information stopped coming in and the murder squad stood down and moved on to new enquiries concerning other matters.

Richard Gibson's family identified and claimed his body and buried him in his home town of Carluke. He had left there 25 years previously, to make his way, and hopefully his fortune, in the world. It all ended when this quiet and shy man suffered a brutal and savage death.

The last part of this trilogy of murder has, by the very nature of the subject, a familiar ring to it. Two patrolling policemen, walking their beat, found themselves in North Carriage Drive, one of the main thoroughfares of Glasgow Green, about 11.15pm on Thursday 28th January 1960. It was a bitterly cold night and got colder as the night progressed.

As they walked and talked, their attention was drawn to a male lying in the roadway. At first they thought that it must be a drunk, who only needed to be lifted to his feet and sent on his way. As they neared him, even in the dark, they could see blood seeping from beneath the body and leaking onto the roadway. An ambulance and other officers were summoned to the scene. The man, Arthur Gordon Still, was barely alive. He had been stabbed numerous times on both his body and neck. The ambulance whisked him off to the nearby Royal Infirmary, but he died shortly after arriving there, without ever regaining consciousness and therefore, without speaking to police.

Very quickly, police sealed off Glasgow Green in an attempt to trap Still's killer. Before midnight, police were conducting full-scale searches in the park and surrounding area. It was one of those searches which turned up an unusual aspect to this case. Seventeen-year-old James McMahon from nearby Baltic Street in the Calton area of the city, was found in Rutherglen Road. McMahon was suffering from multiple stab wounds to his body and literally collapsed into the arms of the police officers who had found him. He was rushed to the Victoria Infirmary.

Despite an all-night search, police could not discover any culprit or weapon that might have been used. Obviously, the police considered that the best lead they had would be the evidence or statement made by McMahon, but in reality, McMahon was saying very little, apart from the fact that he could not remember anything about the attack on him or his movements prior to it. Medical examinations showed that Still and McMahon had been stabbed with a similar type knife – one which had a stiletto type blade.

Once again, police appealed for help in tracing Still's movements on the Thursday night. He was a 36-year-old single man who worked as a merchant seaman and resided in Elderpark Street, Govan. He had only landed back in Glasgow on the Wednesday morning after a four-month voyage. The police appeal fell on deaf ears. Not one person came forward to assist the inquiry. One of the few things McMahon could or would say to police was that he had been in Glasgow Green, using it as a short-cut, and after being stabbed, made his way across the suspension bridge and into Rutherglen Road, where he was found. McMahon could or would not illuminate to police any further. He claimed not to have seen his attacker.

Very soon, the police inquiry ground to a halt as information and clues dried up. It seemed to some police officers that the public's apathy to murder was growing with each reported incidence of it.

Was there a serial killer who was using Glasgow Green as his hunting ground? All habitual criminals, murderers or otherwise, have a particular style, or modus operandi. They are creatures of habit. A housebreaker will use the same screwdriver, a murderer the same gun, knife or whatever. Very rarely will the criminal change his habits. It is these patterns that help police identify when one person is responsible for more than one crime, or a series of crimes.

In all three cases detailed in this chapter, there are a great number of similarities. The police had so many similar unanswered questions in each case it is surprising it took them until the final murder to realise that all three were linked. Or maybe, as is more likely, it was only after the last murder that they made their own theories public. Even so, the majority of the questions raised by the individual cases were never satisfactorily answered.

All three men were attacked during the hours of darkness and stabbed on the body and neck with a similar weapon, thought to be a knife with a stiletto blade. Robbery was obviously not the motive for the attacks, as all three men had money and identification on them, making it easy for police to quickly identify them. But what was the motive for the murders? Why were three men in a park late at night, miles from their respective homes when the park was not en route to their homes? What was James McMahon's involvement in all of this? Why was he unable, or unwilling, to give a description, even a partial one, of his attacker or attackers? Could there have been a sexual background to these murders? Two of the three victims were unmarried while the third had been separated from his wife for a considerable period of time. Was McMahon part of a classic 'honey-trap' involving prostitutes that had gone wrong? Or could he have been part of a homosexual tryst? Only McMahon knew for sure, and he would not, or could not, say.

There is a gap in time between the first and second murders of almost two years. This could infer that the killer had an enforced break, maybe being sentenced to a period of imprisonment for some other crime. Or maybe, he was never away from the scene. Perhaps he had continued with his attacks, but none of his assaults resulted in death. If there was a sexual element to these acts of violence, and there is a strong suggestion that there was, it is possible that the victims, injured or otherwise, would not have wished to report these matters to the authorities for fear of having to answer the obvious awkward questions.

Whoever was stalking Glasgow Green wasn't alone in his ideas. James Denovan and his cohorts were doing something similar across the city in Queens Park in 1960. When they were arrested, they were quizzed for hours regarding the murders in Glasgow Green, but were never charged. There were just too many differences to suggest involvement by them.

Whatever the motives behind the murders one thing is for sure. The three murdered men came face to face with a vicious and, some might say, professional killer.

A killer that, to this day, remains undetected.

Chapter 25
Queens Park, April 1960

Only a couple of months had elapsed since the last murder on Glasgow Green when another killing occurred in a different Glasgow public park. At first, it wasn't classed as a crime. It was listed as a death due to natural causes. John Thomson, who gave his address as 16 Perth Road, Dundee, booked a room at the Parkview Hotel, Queen's Drive, Glasgow in the late afternoon of Wednesday 6th April 1960. He told the receptionist, Mabel Sheard, that he was attending an international football match at Hampden Park that night. Indeed, the football match did take place that night – Scotland vs England, which ended in a 1-1 draw – but whether Thomson attended the match or not is unknown because his dead body was found in bushes, in Queen's Park Recreation Ground by a late-night dog walker, not long after the final whistle had gone.

Police were called to the scene and initially Thomson's death was treated as having occurred through natural causes. The fact that the deceased man had a fractured skull at the rear, just at the base, was put down to him striking his head on the ground when he collapsed.

The body was removed to the city mortuary and it was there that police found a receipt in the name of 'Thomson' from the Parkview Hotel. A quick call was made there and police were able to confirm the dead man's identity. However, all this began to unravel when Glasgow police got word back from their Dundee counterparts that no John Thomson was known at the Perth Road address. In an effort to identify the corpse, Glasgow police took its fingerprints. In the meantime, and following standard procedures, police issued an appeal for any relatives of a 50-year-old male found dead in the park from natural causes to come forward. The appeal was printed in one newspaper only, the *Daily Record* of 7th April 1960.

No one ever did come forward but within days, the result came back that the fingerprints belonged to one John Cremin, a small-time criminal from Glasgow. Although Cremin was a petty crook, his occupation was listed as 'general dealer'. He was also a transient who had no fixed address. But what had he been doing booking into a hotel using a false name? Police were baffled and remained so for a number of months.

Over the next few months a number of men were attacked and robbed while in Queen's Park recreation ground. The modus operandi appeared to be quite simple; attack the victim from behind by jumping on their back and knocking or forcing them to the ground. Once on the ground, the victim's pockets would be rifled and his valuables stolen. If the victim offered resistance in any form, he would find himself being threatened with large knives.

In the Britain of that time, homosexuality, whether in public or private, was a crime and Queen's Park recreation ground was well known as a haunt of homosexuals. One of the park's attractions was the fact that it was unfenced and therefore open to all, 24 hours a day. Locals would not venture into the park grounds for fear of being accosted or of being seen by others and wrongly considered to be homosexual.

The police were responsive to the problems in and around the park. However, what the police were not fully aware of was the extent of the number of assaults and robberies that were taking place in the park grounds. Apart from a few men who had come forward to complain of being attacked, locals had constantly voiced their fears about the dangers that could be found there after dark. In an effort to rid the area of the unwanted and illegal homosexual element, police placed the park's public toilets under discreet surveillance. On the evening of 11th August 1960, James Denovan was arrested along with a number of other men who had been present in the toilets.

Once back at the police office, Denovan was searched and a newspaper cutting was found in his wallet. Suspicions about this item were aroused immediately among detectives, as it was considered an 'odd' possession for a 16-year-old boy to have. The cutting related to the plea for relatives of Cremin to come forward to the police. Although questioned about the cutting, Denovan never elaborated on his reasons for having it. Denovan appeared at court, charged with engaging in an indecent act in the public toilet and, such was the seriousness of the alleged offence, he was sent to a remand home to await trial on the charge.

It was during his time on remand that Denovan admitted to his father, during one visit, that he and his 19-year-old friend Anthony Joseph Miller, had attacked and robbed Cremin. Although he didn't believe his son, Mr Denovan telephoned the police and informed them of the nature of his conversation with his son. James Denovan was interviewed at length (over three days) and he explained about the newspaper cutting of the plea for missing relatives and how it came to be in his possession. He had kept the cutting in his wallet and over the course of the summer months, showed it off to various friends.

Denovan subsequently made a voluntary statement, in the presence of his father, and in which he incriminated Miller and himself in the murder of Cremin and the assaults and robberies of others. The substance of Denovan's statement was that, along with Miller, they would go along to Queen's Park recreation ground in the late evening. Denovan would then go into the public toilets there and would engage men in conversation. These men would usually suggest homosexual acts to Denovan, who would always counter the suggestion with the proposal to go elsewhere in the park, and always to a place much quieter than the toilets.

With the idea accepted, Denovan and his soon-to-be victim would leave the toilet block and en-route to their agreed location, Miller, and on occasions, another youth, would appear and assault the victim by knocking him to the ground. The victim would be robbed of any valuables and frequently, threatened with a knife.

When asked, Denovan told the detectives that he and Miller only preyed on homosexuals. The rationale behind their thinking was two-fold. They were easy victims because they seldom fought back and because there was little chance of getting caught as they very rarely reported this type of incident to the police, for obvious reasons.

In the case of John Cremin, the initial meeting took place in the lavatory, but very quickly, Cremin attempted to touch Denovan in a sexual manner. Denovan backed away and directed Cremin that if he wanted to continue, then it would have to be elsewhere. As he and Cremin walked along a pathway, they passed Miller, who was staggering and pretending to be drunk. It is possible that having seen Miller, Cremin became suspicious or anxious at this point, but Denovan reassured him by saying, 'Ignore him. He's drunk.'.

Almost as soon as they had passed, Miller stopped his acting and struck a massive blow to the back of Cremin's head with a large piece of wood. Because of the size of the lump of timber, Miller needed to use both hands to wield it. Cremin fell forward on to his face on the tarmacadam pathway and Miller and Denovan rifled his pockets.

Denovan claimed that when they turned Cremin over the first time, it was only to get easier access to his valuables, and that their victim was still breathing at this time. Miller found a penknife in one pocket and used it to hack at the other pockets, especially those in Cremin's overcoat. Both attackers then turned Cremin over again and Denovan removed a wad of bank notes from the hip pocket of their victim's trousers. Miller removed Cremin's wristwatch. Once satisfied that they had taken everything of value, they ran off and when safely away from the park, checked to see what their haul was – £67 in notes, a penknife, a watch and a bank book. The notes were shared equally and Miller retained possession of the remaining items.

Denovan also claimed that the day after Cremin's murder, when he went to Miller's home, Miller asked for the return of the stolen bank notes Denovan had been given. Miller's reasoning was that the bank notes were newly issued and the serial numbers ran in sequential order, therefore making them easier to trace. Miller burned all but £7 of the £67. All of this seemed too easy for Miller and Denovan and they continued to frequent the popular park, Glasgow's oldest. They attacked quite a number of men over the next few months, albeit during the hours of darkness only.

There is a thread of thinking that Miller and Denovan did not run away immediately after the robbery, as Denovan suggested, but that they had a few kicks at Cremin's face, head and body, possibly in retribution for Cremin's minor sexual assault on Denovan in the public toilet. Cremin's body was found to have a number of minor cuts and abrasions, which had originally been put down to his falling on the hard footpath. A review of the injuries, in light of the new information of Denovan's confession, led to the new conclusion. However, during the subsequent trial, this particular point wasn't laboured in any great detail.

Detectives called at the home of 19-year-old apprentice cabinetmaker Anthony Miller, at 351 Calder Street, Govanhill, Glasgow, and arrested him. Together, Miller and Denovan appeared at court, charged with the capital murder of John Cremin and three further charges of assault and robbery. And so they languished in custody until their trial started in the North Court at the High Court of Justiciary in Glasgow on Monday 14th November 1960. Lord Wheatley presided over the trial and the courtroom was packed each day.

Three men gave evidence at the start of the trial. Dr James McKay told the court that he was attacked by three youths as he used the park as a shortcut to get to his home at 120 Hickman Street, Govanhill. A knife was pressed against his throat and he was warned not to make any noise. His watch and cash were taken from him and, just as his assailants were about to run off, one stopped and tore his spectacles from his face. Then they ran away.

Another witness, 35-year-old Robert Easdale, claimed he was attacked by three young men with a knife. He tried to run away but his legs gave way and he fell to the ground. He had collapsed because he had been stabbed in the chest. He spent six weeks in hospital with head and chest injuries.

Another male, 30-year-old Douglas Nicholl, parked his car in Queen's Drive and entered the park in order to attend at the Queen's Park Tennis Club and was attacked by three youths. Again, the victim was robbed of his wristwatch, cash and keys. A knife was waved in his face and he was threatened. After the youths ran away, Nicholl found that he still had some loose change in his pocket and he took a bus to his home in Busby. Once there, he telephoned police, but only to inform them that his motorcar would be parked all night in Queen's Drive. He made no mention whatsoever of the assault on him.

There are a few inconsistencies in Nicholl's tale. There is no doubt he was attacked and robbed but after this occurred and his attackers had run off, why did he not continue to the Tennis Club for immediate assistance? With his car keys stolen, Nicholl got a bus home and told police about his car being in Queen's Drive but nothing about the assault. Even viewing Nicholl's actions 50 almost years later, they appear to suggest that Nicholl was hiding something.

Of the three witnesses, only Dr McKay was able (or willing) to identify any assailants, and even then, it was only a partial identification of Miller. Next came a procession of the accused youths' young friends. Crawford Mure, James Sinclair, James Beattie, Arthur Phillips, Kenneth Williams and George Orr, all but one of whom was 16 years of age. All of them told of how they were present at various times and places, when the story of Cremin's murder was recounted by either Denovan or Miller, or both, and of how the newspaper cutting was passed around for everyone to read.

The second day of the trial started with a change of plea from both Miller and Denovan. Both now admitted to the three charges of assault and robbery and the trial continued. The case for the Crown had concluded and it was now the turn of the defence. Denovan gave evidence in his defence. He would be the only defence witness to be called. He proceeded to relate to a hushed courtroom the full contents of his voluntary statement. He detailed how he was used as a decoy, where he entered the toilets in the park, met with older men there and suggested to them moving outside to somewhere quieter. On the premise, spoken or otherwise, of illicit sexual activity, they complied, and then, when out of the view of others, the men were attacked, threatened and robbed.

The morning of Wednesday 16th November was spent in summing up by all involved. The advocate-depute, for the Crown, told the jury that he did not wish for them to convict James Denovan of capital murder. He argued that the evidence that had been heard in the case showed that Denovan did not use any violence against Cremin, but he had still taken an active part in the murder. The jury were absent for all of 35 minutes before returning and announcing a unanimous guilty verdict against both accused, although the jury took note of the legal advice given to them and found only Miller guilty of capital murder. The courtroom was silent as Lord Wheatley pronounced his sentence on both accused.

Denovan was ordered to be detained during Her Majesty's pleasure. Female members of the jury could be heard sobbing quietly as the judge turned his attention to Miller. There was only one sentence that could be handed down and Lord Wheatley put the black cap on as he read out his proclamation. Neither Miller nor Denovan seemed moved by their fate and both were led down to the cells below without any incident.

Immediately, the respective legal teams began preparations for appeals against the convictions of both youths. As a consequence of the appeals, the execution date of 7th December was postponed and by a strange quirk of fate, that is the date on which the appeals were heard at the Scottish Criminal Appeal Court in Edinburgh. Both appeals centred on the basis that the verdict of the jury was contradictory to the evidence led in the case. Miller's appeal also added that there had been a misdirection of the jury by the presiding judge.

The appeals of both youths were dismissed by the Appeal Court as being 'completely devoid of substance'. The three Appeal Court judges (Lords Clyde, Carmont and Guthrie) agreed unanimously that both accused displayed 'a callous disregard' for the consequence of their violent actions. A new execution date was fixed for 22nd December 1960.

As soon as it was known that the appeals had failed, a petition was started for the reprieve of Miller. Mrs Alice Cullen, MP for Gorbals, started it all off and she managed to get 58 other MPs and three peers to sign it. The petition found additional support from those who had previously been advocating an amendment to the Criminal Justice Bill. The modification they sought would see the minimum age for hanging raised from 18 to 21 years of age. On Monday 19th December, the Secretary of State for Scotland, Mr John Maclay, refused the request for the reprieve of Miller. He would hang as arranged, in four days' time.

The decision caused a major outcry when it was pointed out that he had, three days earlier, granted a reprieve to Robert McKenna Cribbes Dickson

(25), who had been found guilty of the capital murder of his fellow lighthouse keeper on Little Ross Island in the Solway Firth earlier in 1960. Critics argued that Dickson was guilty of premeditated murder whilst Miller's case was not as clear-cut. In hindsight, there was ample justification for that argument, but even so, the Secretary of State's decision stood.

Just before eight am on Thursday 22nd December 1960, while most Glasgow folk were more concerned about the approach of Christmas, Anthony Joseph Miller was escorted from his cell to the gallows. Only three people had gathered outside Barlinnie and stood in silence on a bitterly cold morning as the black flag was raised above the prison walls just minutes later.

The small turnout made a mockery of the arrangements made by Glasgow police in closing off the road leading to the prison gates and putting on extra officers to deal with anticipated large crowds. Perhaps, after all the furore surrounding the case and reprieve petitions, the general public had decided that Miller had deserved his punishment?

Postscript

Miller and Denovan were questioned in relation to the unsolved Glasgow Green murders. Very soon into the interviews it became apparent to detectives that they were not responsible for any of those killings.

As a consequence of this case, Queens Park Recreation Ground was completely fenced in and subject to the rules governing all other Glasgow public parks. Gates opened at dawn and closed at dusk.

Index

Index

The Book of Glasgow Murders